Radical Pursuit

A Young Adult's Guide to Following Jesus

ABBY ROBERSON

Published by KHARIS PUBLISHING, imprint of
KHARIS MEDIA LLC.

Copyright © 2018 Abby Roberson

Cover design by Julia Bentley and Isaac Grothe

ISBN-13: 978-1-946277-11-4
ISBN-10:1-946277-11-8

All KHARIS PUBLISHING products are available at
special quantity discounts for bulk purchase for sales
promotions, premiums, fund-raising, and educational
needs. For details, write:

Kharis Media LLC
709 SW Elmside Drive
Bentonville, AR 72712

Tel: 1-479-599-8657
info@kharispublishing.com
www.kharispublishing.com

KHARIS PUBLISHING

DEDICATION

Dedicated to my friends and family in Ohio who are tangled in my heart and who I had in mind while creating this book.

ACKNOWLEDGMENTS

The Leader Scholars Institute (LSI) at John Brown University: Thank you Becci Rothfuss, Corrie Wimberly, and LSI student directors for everything you do for LSI. I would not have been motivated to start this project without the foundation that you all laid for me. Thank you, Becci, for helping me in the initial stages of constructing my idea and treating it as attainable.

The Bentley's: Thank you for the hospitality and support you have shown me during this process. You made me feel like the work I was doing was worthy and important. I am eternally grateful for your encouragement, prayers, and coffee supply. Thank you, Tina and Julia, for dedicating time and effort to proofread and edit my work.

CONTRIBUTORS

Thank you, Dr. Lanker, for your role as pastoral editor and for always keeping the reader's perspective in mind. Thank you, Melissa Varner, for serving as editor. Thank you, Vanessa Dixon, Dr. David Brisben, Brandon Miller, Kevin Rusack, Dr. Rod Reed, Dr. Lou Cha, and Dr. Ted Song for taking on the heart of this book with your chapter contributions. Thank you, Julia and Isaac, for coming together to make a beautiful cover design for me.

Thank you, Dr Umesiri, for being a great mentor. This book would not exist without you. I appreciate you patiently seeing it through from beginning to end and for always asking, "how is Abby doing?"

Thank you, Kharis Publishing, for agreeing to publish this book before I had even recruited a single author, and for your continued faith in this project.

CONTENTS

My Radical Pursuit
– Abby Roberson

As my contribution to this book, I want to share with you why I chose to create it and a bit of my story.

I am involved in a leadership development program called Leader Scholars Institute (LSI) at the university I attend, John Brown University (JBU). As third-year participants in the LSI program, we have been challenged to create something new or change something that already exists, based on what we have learned thus far in our college experience about ourselves, our strengths, our passions, and our mission. That challenge motivated me to create something that tells of God and His faithfulness to others, because that is at the core of all I have experienced in the past three years of my life. I wanted this project to be something accessible for people who may be outside of the Christian community because before I found myself in it, I had a lot of misconceptions about what it means to be a Christian. Therefore, I have recruited professors, pastors, and teachers to write about things relevant to God and knowing Him, in the hope of pointing the reader toward a relationship with their Maker; the very thing that altered the course of my life.

I have always believed in God, and both sides of my

family have always held Christian beliefs and values but going to church was only an occasional occurrence for me. I was taught at a young age that Jesus died on the cross for my sins, and I accepted that as true. I even got baptized at a church I visited at the age of twelve. However, as I got older and more independent, I began to question how relevant Jesus was to me, and I didn't bother dedicating much time to figure it out. I still believed Christianity to be true and real, but there was a major disconnect between those beliefs and the way I lived my life. Therefore, I doubted whether I was actually saved, and was hesitant to confidently call myself a Christian. I knew that Christians were supposed to be different than the rest of the world, and my outward life did not seem much different than the lives of the non-Christian people I knew. I still went to youth group on and off for a while as a teenager and enjoyed it. However, my desire to act in ways that were viewed as wrong in Christianity outweighed my desire to be acquainted with Jesus. I felt hypocritical and guilty about doing both, so I soon decided to stop attending church all together. By the age of seventeen, I had stopped thinking much about God and the church, and my life lacked hope in anything greater than what I could control. I never denounced my belief in the sacrifice Jesus made for my sin, or in the existence of God, but I still wasn't entirely convinced that I should care enough to change how I was living for it. I was a highly social and occupied person, so I just lived my life the way I thought it was okay to live it. I only prayed when I was scared, and my biggest fear was dying before I got the chance to get on good terms with God. However, those thoughts could eventually be pushed to the back of my mind. No fear of death and Hades, and no lecture from my Papaw was enough to cause me to decide to get back into church and follow Jesus, which honestly seemed very unappealing to me at the time. It wasn't until I was eighteen years old that I began to recognize the need for God in my life, and it wasn't until I started following Jesus' teaching at nineteen years old that my life changed.

My salvation story really begins in the fall of 2013 when I started college. I was in my first semester of college at Miami University in Ohio, and among other courses, I was taking microbiology, geology, anatomy, and physiology. I wasn't looking for an eye-opening epiphany when I enrolled in these classes; I was just a freshman who was working part time and trying to get my basics out of the way. However, as I began studying these subjects, I became fully convinced that there was someone much more wonderful and powerful than me who created it all. The things I was learning about in the natural world were incredible, and I found them to be too orderly and purposeful to have happened by chance alone. Through this contemplation, God started to seem less like a daunting authority figure who wanted me to go to church, and more like someone who had created an amazing work of art. I can remember looking up at the moon and the stars one night after work, sometime near the end of that semester, and feeling a sense wonder about God for the first time. It seemed that everything in my life was overlapping and pointing me to the need to know this creative God. But I knew that God was the God of the Bible, and I still wasn't sure that I was ready, or able, to become a true Christian. Regardless of the doubts and the ponderings I had, I think back on that time as being spent in admiration of God as He was revealing Himself to me through His artistic hand in creation.

Following that semester, during winter break in 2014, I began having serious convictions for the first time in my life. Meaning that, I started feeling bad when I acted in the ways that I always recognized as wrong but that I had never actually *felt* wrong about up to that point. I became so convicted that I tried to quit doing a lot of those things I had done so easily before, and by before, I mean the things I had done earlier that week, or even that day. The conviction I felt was strong, and the call to know the One who placed it there was too pressing to ignore. I began to question the direction my life was headed; I was realizing how limited and unsatisfying the things my life revolved around were, and how incapable I was at redirecting my life on my own. All my life I believed in God and looking back I see that He was calling me to live like it. I felt that I needed to do something in response to all that was occurring, and for me that meant making a serious change.

Near the end of the spring semester during my freshman year at Miami University, I called my dad, who lived in Arkansas with his second family, and asked him if I could transfer to a school there and live with them. I felt a change in my physical environment would help me to make the other life changes that I wanted to make. It was too difficult to for me to make those changes and live the Christian life in a place that I had spent so many years doing just the opposite. I wanted a fresh start. I wanted to get involved in the church and learn more about God through His Word, but I wasn't sure how to begin that journey on my own. So, I figured moving to a new place and being around Christians like my family members in Arkansas, who were stronger in their faith than I was, would help get me on the right path. As I explained all of this to my dad, he suggested I apply to John Brown University (JBU), the Christian college not too far from where they lived. I loved his suggestion, and I decided to act on it. It didn't take long for every detail to line up so that I could transfer from Miami in Ohio to JBU in Arkansas. I was sad to leave the school, workplace, friends, and family members that I had just grown to truly appreciate, but there was no way I could have abandoned the secure plans that were falling into place for me to move. Although I didn't know it at the time, I can now see that it all happened so effortlessly because I was acting according to God's plan for my life. God was putting me on the track to meet Him.

During the summer of 2014, as I wrapped up my time in Ohio and eagerly prepared to move to Arkansas to attend JBU, I continued to strive to do all the right things, but I often failed. I couldn't wait to get to JBU where I imagined changing would be much easier. I believed that God had great things in store for me there, and I couldn't wait to find out what they were. However, when I finally arrived at JBU in the fall, I didn't experience any sudden changes and my life did not automatically become so much better like I thought. Although I loved being at my new school, I often found myself frustrated that my problems and discontentment did not stay behind Ohio. I began comparing myself to other JBU students, most of whom had grown up steadily in the church, and I thought, "This is where you have to come from to be a solid Christian? I'm in trouble." I lost the optimism I had in the summer, and I started doubting God's interest in me considering how I had lived my life up to that point. I didn't know many Old Testament Bible stories, I didn't know what the doxology was, and I didn't have a mission trip experience to talk about. It seemed like I was so far behind everyone else, and even though I was surrounded by so many, I actually felt more alone that ever.

Though in the moment I often only saw my struggles, looking back I can see that I encountered a lot of people who did a good job of brightening my days. I came across JBU professors and staff members who not only cared about my performance in my classes, but also about my overall well-being. I met other students who treated me with kindness and called me friend. A lot of people I crossed paths with spoke simple truths of Christianity to me, unaware that it was my first time hearing it. I joined a group of upper classmen who welcomed me to go camping with them, and that was my first time having fun sitting around a campfire without using any substances to do so. I also became very close with my roommate who took a genuine interest in me, my life, and my relationship with God. She set an example for me of what it means to live for God, and she helped me to understand His grace and His love for me. Through talking with her, I realized I wasn't the only one who felt alone, so she and I, along and a few others we had met, became dedicated to driving to church together every Sunday morning. The biblical teachings I heard in church, along with the life-giving conversations that followed, were refreshing, enjoying, and something I had never experienced before. At the bottom of our church's pamphlet that they gave out every Sunday was a note that read, "Be doers of the word, and not hearers only," which is a verse in the Bible from James 1:22. Still struggling to be content, I thought I would give that a try, and I found that it was reshaping my life.

In addition to the people I encountered and the church body that I became a part of, the New Testament class that I was taking that semester had a tremendous impact on my life. As required reading, I read the gospels of Jesus for the first time. As I read them, I often found myself admiring the character and life of Jesus. My eyes were opening to God's glory just as they were months back when I was a freshman at Miami. Only this time, instead of having wonder towards God through studying His creation, I was falling in love with God through studying His Son, Jesus. I read how Jesus befriended sinners and how He loved the lost, the broken, and the lowly. I learned that He wasn't an angry or grudge-holding God, but a God full of compassion, mercy, and grace. I remember reading the story of how Jesus handled the woman who was caught in adultery with such love and cleverness, and I thought, "*This* man is who Christians serve? I understand why!" My concerns of feeling far behind my peers began to fade, and I was officially no longer indifferent about Jesus. A deep desire to know Him, follow Him, and be like Him was placed inside my heart. For the first time in my life, I spent a great deal of time reading the

Bible, and I felt like I had found buried treasure. I continued to do what was written at the bottom of our church's pamphlet; I not only heard and read the Word, but I put it into action. Even when I didn't feel close to Him, I continued to press on as I obeyed and believed His Word. The more time I spent getting to know Him, the more I found Him, and the more I was united with Him. The more I was united with Him, the more He changed me, and the more I wanted to know Him. It was an upward spiral, and I was all in. As silly as it sounds, I repeated the words, "I am a Christian," aloud to myself all the time, so that I could confidently own my new identity and help my actions to follow. What I like to say about this time in my life is that I ran, I jumped, and I was caught. I wasn't trying to do all the right things or avoid all the wrong things. I just committed my life to following Jesus' way, which was finally what I desired more than anything else.

God's Word proved true, and He made it clear to me multiple times that I was on the right track as I made Jesus the center of my life. As I continued to seek, find, and live for Jesus, I came to a moment of understanding that there was nothing that had happened in my life that could keep me from Him because of the sacrifice He made for all of my sins through His undeserved death on the cross and His resurrection from the grave. I felt His love for me and I was fully satisfied. In response to the amazing grace that found me in that ordinary moment, I surrendered my past, my present, and my future. I said in my heart, "All I am is Yours," for I had discovered that he is worthy of my praise, my trust, and my life, which made me want to give those things to Him. In obedience to God's Word, I was baptized the following spring semester in February 2015 as an outward expression of the change that happened to me internally. This time I meant it.

The change that God made in me did not come from me passively waiting for it to happen, and it wasn't just a surface level change—how I spend my weekends. That type of change is barely worth mentioning in comparison to the deep change He made in my innermost being through connecting my life to His. He changed who I serve, from myself to Him, and therefore others. He changed my thought pattern; especially regarding myself and other people. I no longer think of others lightly, but as people of intrinsic value who were purposely created by God. This new perspective makes compassion and kindness come a lot more natural, and comparison a lot more foreign. God also changed what I ultimately hope in, from gaining love that comes from a person to having perfect love that comes from Him. He helps me find peace in my anxieties, struggles, and circumstances, not peace that comes from having a plan, but peace that comes from knowing and trusting His words and His plans. Having my eyes opened to the way I have been taken in and forgiven helps me to do the same to others. Once I talk to God and recite scripture to myself instead of replaying my own thoughts in my head, I can rest easy knowing that He will ultimately resolve and heal any painful circumstance. And when I don't know what else to do, I know I can follow His example and He will lead me. Through losing my life to Jesus, I have found my life in a far more meaningful way than ever before.

As true and wonderful as all of that is, I also do not want to give the impression that the changes God made in me were quick and pain-free, or that I am now perfect, and my life is easier since making the decision to commit my life to God. Since becoming a Christian, I have still been faced with challenges, adversity, heartbreak, and consequences of regrettable decisions. However, I have come to learn that it is not about me and what I do, but about God and what He does. He never ceases to hold my hand as He guides me with His counsel, even in my worst weaknesses and struggles. Though it doesn't always seem like it, my ongoing journey as a Christian is both glorious and beautiful; not because it features me, but because it features God. There is no turning back on my eternal decision to enter a relationship with Him. However, I must continuously battle myself and my tendencies to trust what the world says, with all its empty attraction. Over the past three wild years, God has taught me, changed me, and has given me purpose as I do the work He has laid before me. When I have found myself lost and waited upon Him, He has never failed to show me the way. He has given me wisdom in messy situations and has always led me to where or to whom I should go. He was the one I needed in my youth, the one whom I sought in the beginning of my adulthood, the one whom I found in Jesus, and the one whom I choose to turn to even today as I sit in a home that is not my own and sing the glory of His name, proclaiming, "How awesome are your deeds!"

What I want you to know is that I am not special. Since spending three years involved with things that go along with the Christian lifestyle, I now know the words to the doxology. I know a lot of Old Testament Bible stories. I have been on a couple mission trips, and my church attendance is steadier than ever. But none of those things qualify me for a relationship with God, just like they didn't qualify my Christian peers as I once thought. They are things that I want to be a part of in response to the new life God has given me. They aren't sufficient for knowing Jesus as my savior.

So, whether you find yourself close to things related to the Christian lifestyle or as far away as it gets, Jesus promises that you who were once far off have been brought near by his death on the cross (Eph. 2:13). If you have been wanting a relationship with God but have failed to find your way, I invite you to do what I did. Seek Him out. Don't give up. Don't try to clean up your life on your own. Begin talking to God, and to others you know who have faith in Him, about whatever doubts you may have, and in whatever situation you find yourself in. Hang around people who are stronger in their faith than you are. Place yourself in environments where you are hearing biblical truths. Cling to God's word as your anchor; ask Him for help. If you lose your life for Christ's sake, you will surely find it.

> "Therefore, I tell you, do not be anxious about your life, what you will eat or what you will drink, nor about your body, what you will put on. Is life not more than food and the body more than clothing? Look at the birds of the air: they neither sow nor reap nor gather into barns, and yet your heavenly Father feeds them. Are you not of more value than they? And which of you by being anxious can add a single hour to his lifespan? And why are you anxious about clothing? Consider the lilies of the field, how they grow: they neither toil nor spin, yet I tell you, even Solomon in all his glory was not arrayed like one of these. But if God so clothes the grass of the field, which today is alive and tomorrow is thrown into the oven, will he not much more clothe you, O you of little faith? Therefore, do not be anxious saying, 'What shall we eat?' or 'What shall we drink?' or 'What shall we wear?' For the Gentiles seek after these things, and your heavenly Father knows that you need them all. But seek first the kingdom of God and His righteousness, and all these things will be added to you."
> Matt. 6:25-33

Jesus' "I Am" Statements
– Vanessa Dixon

Chances are, you've heard of it. Even if you did not grow up in church, it would probably ring a bell of familiarity. John 3:16, the most quoted scripture in the Bible. We see it plastered on billboards, at football games, on people's cars, t-shirts, and more. If you have grown up in church, you most likely can quote it without batting an eye. It has become so familiar that many don't even give it a second thought. It says, "For God so loved the world that He gave his only begotten Son, that whoever believes in Him should not perish but have everlasting life." What a great verse! This one short verse has brought hope and salvation to countless people. I was one that grew up in a great church, but I had personally become all too familiar with this scripture. I mean really, once you have said a prayer and gotten your "ticket to heaven," you're good, right? Isn't that what this scripture means? God's love was so great for us that He gave His Son to die for us so we could go to heaven, right? Wrong!

Let me challenge you to think differently about this verse. One day, when I was reading the Bible, I read John 17, a passage where Jesus is praying. In his prayer, he gives us a key to unlock a truth about eternal life. John 17:3 says, "And this is eternal life, that they may know You, the only true God, and Jesus Christ whom You have sent." What Jesus said is the definition of what eternal (or everlasting) life is. Notice that he didn't say, "And this is eternal life, that when they die, they can go to heaven." So then, what is eternal life? That we can *know* the only true God and Jesus Christ. Know Him. When that definition of eternal life gets put back into John 3:16, there is a whole new meaning. God loved us so much that He sent His only begotten Son, and whoever believes in Him will not perish but can know Him! The whole reason God sent Jesus to live and die for us was not to give us a "ticket to heaven." It was to reveal God's character and make a way for us to have a very personal relationship with Him. He loved us so much that He was willing to pay a high price so that we could know Him today and always. Enjoying eternal life doesn't just mean living forever in Heaven. Eternal life starts as soon as you enter a relationship with Him, and it lasts forever!

Here is something else to consider. If God loved us so much that He sent His only Son so that we would not perish, but we could know Him, then what does it mean to perish? I always thought that perishing meant going to hell and everlasting life meant going to heaven. But, if everlasting life means having a relationship with Him starting now, then perishing must mean the death that comes from not experiencing that relationship with Him. Quite a different perspective! I do believe there is a heaven and hell, and we do have a choice in the matter, but there is so much emphasis on what happens after we die that we forget about what we can experience here on earth. There is so much life to experience now by having that personal relationship with Him.

I have been married to my husband for more than fifteen years now, and we have three amazing children. You know how our relationship developed? We started to spend time together. Sometimes it was in a group with other people, and sometimes it was just us talking, listening, and simply being with each other. The more I got to know him and spend time with him, the more I fell in love with him and wanted to spend more time with him. The same is true today. Fifteen years later, I still want to spend time with him. We call each other, hang out together, spend time together, and I continue to discover things about him that I love! There was and is no formula behind it. We didn't commit to spending thirty minutes a day together and then not even talk until the next day. We didn't decide we would see each other only once a week for a couple of hours and then wait until the following week to start the process over. We just wanted to be with each other. We ate together, shopped together, rode together, talked on the phone, etc. Any chance we got, we wanted to include the other. When we try to make a relationship into a formula, it becomes an obligation, one more thing to check off our list for the day. When my relationship with God consists of reading the Bible for thirty minutes a day or going to church on Sundays for a couple of hours, I have to consider that there might not be much of a relationship. It becomes just another thing to check off of my to-do list, so I can move on to the next thing. Relationship, by definition, is a connection. It could be a business relationship or a marriage relationship. There are different levels of relationships that exist. Business relationships tend to have a connection based on what you can do for me or what I can do for you. If one of those conditions doesn't pan out, the business relationship is terminated. Marriage relationships become quite a bit more intimate. You connect in much deeper ways. You enter into a relationship not solely based on what the other can do for you, but you commit to love them and stand by them through anything. When Jesus came so we could have a relationship with Him, it was in pursuit of a marriage relationship. A relationship that is so intimate that you know Him and He knows you in a way that no one else does. He knows the places of your heart and your soul that no one else sees, and you know His heart, what He loves and what He hates. It is a relationship where you are each in constant pursuit of the other and where you want to spend time together. Not just thirty minutes a day, or two hours on a Sunday. We are constantly pursuing each other. James 4:8 says, "Draw near to God and He will draw near to you."

The best way to develop a relationship with someone is to get to know them. When you spend enough time with someone, you learn things about them that make you want to either spend more time with them and pursue a relationship, or run the other way! The greatest way to develop a relationship with God is to spend time with Him. Through that you begin to understand His heart, His love for others, and His many other attributes. A great way to spend time with Him and learn more about Him is through His Word, the Bible. In my pursuit of God, I read His words and study Him and fall more in love with Him. There are things He says and does that cause me to want to know why. It makes me want to better understand His heart and how everything He does is motivated by love. In the book of John, Jesus uses different terms to describe Himself so we can better understand who He is, and how He loves us. These have been referred to as the "I Am" statements.

The first statement Jesus uses in John is in chapter six. He says, "I am the bread of life. He who comes to me shall never hunger, and he who believes in me shall never thirst." I think you would agree that we are hungry people. We crave certain foods and will go to almost any extent to fulfill that craving. Our hunger, though, goes way beyond food. We are a people that hunger physically, spiritually, and emotionally. We look to different people or things to fulfill our hungers and desires, but they never seem to satisfy completely. We have so many options for everything, and yet there are those that walk around completely unfulfilled and still searching. Why is that? It is because they have not come across the one thing that satisfies in a way that nothing else can. When God becomes my one and only, He fulfills all those longings, needs, and desires. I no longer need to look to other people or things to fulfill what He alone provides.

In John 8, Jesus makes another statement about Himself. Jesus spoke again, saying, "I am the light of the world. He who follows me shall not walk in darkness, but have the light of life."

Light is something that makes things visible. Physicist have studied light for years. In fact, the U.S. Department of Energy's website takes thirty-five pages to describe light. That is how complex it is! Light makes it possible for us to see things clearly. It can bring things out in the open that you didn't see before. Only light can dispel darkness. We rely on light more than we realize. Has your power ever gone out and you realize that you need light to accomplish certain things? We try to use other sources of light temporarily, but we are always so thankful when we can have the lights back on. Jesus tells us that He is our light. When we use Him as our light, all other things are made visible. We see direction for our lives clearly, we see areas that need to change, and we see how to handle situations differently. When we try to substitute other lights, they will fail us, and they pale in comparison to the Light of the World.

Moving on to John chapter 10, Jesus reveals that He is the door (or gate). Here, Jesus is referring to His sheep, so some versions use the word "gate." Think about it; a door or a gate gives you access to what is on the other side when it is opened. When Jesus reveals that He is the door, He means that He is the way that we get to what awaits on the other side. Since Adam and Eve disobeyed God in the very beginning, they were separated from the presence of God. From that moment on, things changed for everyone. We were no longer able to be in His presence because sin had caused a divide, and that door was closed. Jesus came to pay the price for our sin and open that door again so, through

Him, we can access the awesome presence of God, and no longer live separated from Him. The heartbreaking truth is that there are those that would rather not walk through the door but are content to let others go through as they watch. Are you content to let others go through while you stand on the sidelines? Jesus paid a high price to open that door for us. Take steps toward the door (Jesus), and you will be drawn to what awaits you on the other side.

In the same chapter, Jesus also reveals that He is the good shepherd, and we are His sheep. There are countless examples throughout scripture of a shepherd's relationship with his sheep. Shepherds don't just go check on their sheep occasionally, they dedicate their life to the sheep. They eat outside with the sheep, sleep outside with the sheep, risk their lives to protect the sheep, and so on. Through this, I can see how overwhelming Jesus' love is for me; He wants to be with me all the time! He gave up his own life to be with me in mine. How can I not love someone who has shown me so much love? A shepherd takes care of every need the sheep have. He finds the best places for them to graze. He doesn't lead his sheep into trouble, but he is always watching over them and protecting them before the sheep even sense danger. The relationship they have is amazing. It demonstrates the incredible unselfishness of the shepherd. There's not a lot in it for him, but he still does it. What a great example of Jesus as our Shepherd.

In John 11, there is a great story where Jesus raises a man from the dead. Through the course of the conversation with the dead man's sister, Jesus reveals that He is the resurrection and the life. If He is resurrection, and He is life, then that means there is no resurrection or life apart from Him. When Jesus died on the cross, death couldn't keep him, because Jesus IS life! He brings life where there is death. Have you had dreams die too early, or hurts that have been buried for so long that you feel a part of you has died? Jesus can cause a broken heart or dream to come alive again.

In John 14, Jesus reiterates some things He has already opened our eyes to see. He says, "I am the way, the truth and the life. No man comes to the Father but by me." We are reminded that Jesus is *the* way, *the* truth, and *the* life. Not *a* way, *a* truth, or *a* life. The only legitimate way to access God, His throne, His presence, a relationship with Him, and all the amazing things He has promised is through Jesus. We must first come through Jesus and understand what He did for us to receive access to God. You may have tried other ways, but have found yourself lost, confused, and misguided. The path Jesus has made for us is a path of truth, a path of life, and a path that provides restoration.

A great way to wrap up these statements Jesus made about Himself is in John 15:5. He says, "I am the vine; you are the branches. If you remain in me and I in you, you will bear much fruit; apart from me you can do nothing." I love this because it all comes back to connection and relationship. If I am a branch, I must be connected to something to be fruitful. I can try all I want, but I will never produce an apple if I am not connected to that tree, but when I am connected, I don't have to try at all. It is a natural thing for fruit that is connected to the life source to be productive. Sometimes we try so hard to be good Christian people and make the right decisions. Say no to all the wrong things and yes to all the right ones. Honestly, doesn't that get stressful sometimes? When I am connected to God through relationship, I am automatically saying yes to the right things, and I don't want any part of other things. It is not all about trying to stay away from wrong things. It's about saying yes to Him and being connected in a relationship with Him. After all, that is why He came.

The Church as Grievous Sinners and Tainted Saints: Experiencing the Community of Grace in the Abraham Story
– David Brisben

In the summer of 1983, I was appointed to cross-cultural mission work under the supervision of the mission board of my Presbyterian denomination. I was assigned to work in the Huasteca, a region in the central east coast states of Mexico, and I would be following the senior missionary who had been in that region for almost 35 years. At the end of a long and productive career, he was going to retire, and my assignment was not so much to replace him as to facilitate the transfer of his extensive mission work to a national Presbyterian body. In his thirty-five years of service, he had started more than thirty churches located in small isolated mountain villages of the Huasteca, a region that was largely populated by a group of indigenous people called the Nahuatl. He had also started a pastoral training center and had several community development projects going in different villages. To say the least, I was excited to be following in the footsteps of this gospel pioneer.

It was not long after arriving that I, along with my wife, Susan, and daughter, Julie, took our first trip up into the mountains to visit one of the Nahuatl villages. We would be staying with the village elder, a man who had been a

Christian for almost thirty years and one of the first Nahuatl converts under the ministry of the senior missionary. We were warmly greeted and treated like royalty, at least as much like royalty as village life could offer.

It was obvious that the people of this village had a deep love for Christ. In the mornings, they often would start the day with community prayer and scripture reading and would end the day the same way. Many days, the elder we were staying with would lead these simple community prayers and scripture readings. Everything was going well, and we continued to be impressed with the spirit-filled love, gentleness, and kindness of these people. Too soon the end of our weeklong visit arrived. On the last evening, as Susan and I were going through our ritual of putting Julie to bed, we began musing over the experiences of the day. That is when I asked Susan if she had figured out who the four different women were that always cooked and ate their meals with us and our host. I simply assumed the oldest looking of the women was his wife but had not figured out the roles of the other three. Susan confessed that she had not figured it out when our daughter Julie spoke up. She connected each of the women with the seven children who were also eating with us. Then, not getting it, I naively mused, I wonder where their fathers are. No sooner had I gotten my question out than Julie answered, naming our host as the father of all the children. When I asked Julie how she knew, our linguistically gifted three-year old said, these two children call this woman mother, these two call that woman mother, these final three call this other woman mother, and none of them call the oldest woman mother. However, they all call our host, the village elder, father. I was astonished and didn't want to believe what I was hearing. How could a man who had been a believer for thirty years be a practicing polygamist? Moreover, how could he be a respected leader in the church? I would soon discover that he was not the only practicing polygamist among the Nahuatl believers. It was an accepted practice in many of their churches.

I was confused, perplexed, and angry. How could these people who call themselves Christians be practicing polygamists? How could they continue to live in sin so openly without any remorse or contrition? When I confronted the senior missionary about this he simply responded that they don't believe it's a sin. He also said that it did not matter that we saw it as sin, they would have to see it as sin if they ever were ever going to turn from it . . . *conviction of sin was the Holy Spirit's job, not ours.* He did not convince me, and I was still determined to bring these Nahuatl Christians to repentance. Two years later, I was back in that same village visiting with a missionary colleague who was there to initiate a community development project. We were meeting with the same village elder who had hosted my family on our first foray into the Huasteca. I decided to confront him about his polygamous marriage. I asked him if he knew that polygamy was sin. He was polite and simply responded that he did not understand why missionaries thought polygamy was sin. He then asked me if I thought God would rather the village women become prostitutes. I said of course not, and he replied, "Then we agree." And that was as far as our conversation went. After that, I had several other conversations with Nahuatl church leaders and village elders about polygamy, but I convinced none that it was sin.

A few years later, my mission board gave me a new assignment. My family and I were moved to central Mexico to the city of San Luis Potosi where I would supervise some new church planting efforts and teach at an interdenominational pastoral training institute called the Center for Theological Studies. At the Center, I was asked not only to teach classes in theology but in marriage and family counseling as well. To say the least, this was a huge learning curve for me. During my first year of teaching, I offered a class on marriage enrichment. Partly because of its newness, and partly because it touched on a felt need in the churches, the class was heavily populated with leaders from Methodist, Presbyterian, Disciples of Christ, Assembly of God, and charismatic Catholic churches. It was an exciting experience, and we got into some very interesting and enlightening discussions. Near the end of the semester, a young man stood up and asked me a question about divorce and remarriage. He wanted to know why American missionaries allowed for remarriage after divorce when Jesus said doing so was adultery. It was not a question I was expecting, and I got pretty defensive. I said that I did not consider remarriage after divorce to be adultery. It was one of those times I wish I would have kept my mouth shut. Immediately a half-dozen other church leaders stood up and challenged me, all quoting Gospel passages (Matt. 19:8-9 and Mark 10:11-12). I asked them how they handled divorce in their churches, and they said they did not allow it. I continued to push them about divorced persons in the church. But for them it was obvious, a divorced person could not remarry and churches that allowed that union were sanctioning adulterous relationships, not marriage. For me, the class that began with such excitement and promise ended with me feeling frustrated and confused.

Later, I began to reflect on my experiences of working and ministering with these Christians from two very different cultural settings. I was the outsider in both cultural settings. Among the Nahuatl in the Huasteca, what was an obvious sin to me, polygamy, was not at all an obvious sin to them. And among the urban Mestizo culture of San Luis Potosi, what was an obvious sin to them was not at all an obvious sin to me. For me, this issue was weighty because of who Christ is as head of the one, holy, catholic church to which we all as believers belong. How could the one, holy, catholic church be holy if we could not even agree on what was sinful? And, how could the one, holy, catholic church be one if we could not even agree on which sinners were to be disciplined? Since those with whom I disagreed believed the Bible to be God's authoritative Word just as I did, I had to ask myself if maybe I was the one incorrectly hearing God speak through His Word.

With the idea that maybe I was the one not correctly hearing God, I returned to the reading and studying of His Word asking for greater clarity and understanding on how to deal with sin in the church. Slowly I started experiencing what I believe was greater clarity from God on this weighty issue (at least weighty for me). In the next few pages, I will try to briefly present how my thinking, attitude, and desires slowly began to be challenged and changed on these issues. God began to challenge and change my understanding on how to deal with sin in the church by teaching me to enter and begin to live out His story, the biblical story. However, since presenting all that entails would require a book, I instead will present how I was challenged and changed by one part of the biblical story, the story of Abraham found in Genesis 12-25.

I am presenting the Abraham story because it is the introductory story to God's redemptive program, the part of His story in which He set in motion His plan and program to redeem and restore all the sin-distorted, broken individuals and families on the earth (Gen. 12:3). God's plan was to begin with Abraham and his family, that is to begin with a sin-distorted, broken individual with a sin-distorted, broken family. After all, Joshua would later remind us that this was not a good Jewish family that God began with, rather, it was a clan of pagan idol-worshippers (Josh. 24:15). Redeeming and restoring this individual and his family and descendants would mean forming them into a community or nation of His people. And through this redeemed and restored community of His people, God would eventually bring about the redemption and restoration of all His creation. Admittedly, this is only the beginning of the story of God's redemptive program, but even in this initial story, God gives us a good picture of how He works His redemption and restoration into sin-distorted, broken individuals and families.

The Abraham story does not actually start with Abraham, but with his father, Terah, who decided to move his family from the region of Ur in southern Mesopotamia to the land of Canaan, a region almost 1,000 miles away (Gen. 11:27). We are not told why Terah decided to make this move, but we do know that cultural decline in Ur led to a large population shift at this time. It is most likely that Terah and his family were part of this population shift.[1] After traveling about 600 of the 1,000 miles to Canaan, Terah and his family stopped in a place called Haran, and there, Terah died (Gen. 11:31-32). This stop in Haran is significant to the story because it is where God first spoke to Abraham promising to make him into a great community, a nation through whom He, God, would bless all the families of the earth. This encounter between God and Abraham is often referred to as Abraham's call because this is the moment when God initiated a covenant relationship, a binding relationship, with him. What was important for me to realize was that Abraham was a seventy-five-year-old pagan Mesopotamian who worshipped the gods of the region of Ur when God called him and entered into this covenant relationship with him. God's promise to bless all the families of the earth through Abraham included God making some other unconditional promises, promises that when fulfilled, would enable Abraham and his descendants to be a blessing to the nations. These other unconditional promises, often called the covenant promises, were to give

[1] James King West, *Introduction to the Old Testament*, (New York: The Macmillan Company, 1971). See also William Lasor, David Hubbard, and Frederic Bush, Old Testament Survey: The Message, Form, and Background of the Old Testament, (Grand Rapids, MI: William B. Eerdmans Publishing Co., 1996), 34-35.

Abraham land, descendants, and protection (Gen. 12:1-3).

These things that I have presented were not new to me. However, the part of the story I previously had ignored was that the original idea to leave Ur and go to Canaan was planted by his unbelieving father, Terah (11:27). As one of my students once pointed out, it takes a lot stronger faith to do something entirely new and different than to continue doing what your father had already been doing. If Abraham's unbelieving father, Terah, as well as hundreds and maybe even thousands of other unbelievers motivated by cultural decline could move their families from Ur to Haran and Canaan, then why should I be so impressed with Abraham for going the final leg of the journey because God called him to do it? And that got my attention only because it helped me to better understand Abraham. I had always thought of Abraham as a man of strong, unwavering faith, the kind of faith I always wanted, the kind of faith I thought was needed to move mountains, or at least to be a truly committed follower of Christ.[2] Consequently, I kept unsuccessfully trying to muster up that kind of faith. And since I was unable to do it, I simply resigned myself to the category of those with a weak and wimpy faith. What I did not realize is that most of us, both ancient believers and modern believers, start this journey with Christ with a weak

---

[2] At this point I should point out that my understanding of Abraham had been more informed by the writer of the book of Hebrews than it had been by the actual story of Abraham in Genesis 12-25. I would venture that the writer of the book of Hebrews did not need to mention Abraham's weak faith when telling his Jewish-Christian audience about Abraham's call simply because his was already familiar with all of Abraham's failings (Heb. 11:1-40). It is the same reason that the writer of Hebrews did not have to talk about the weak faith and failings that are presented in the stories of Sarah, Isaac, Jacob, Gideon, Samson, and Jephthah as well. His audience would have known that the faith displayed by those Old Testament believers was a weak faith that produced as much doubt and disobedience as it did confidence and surety.

faith.

While it is important to realize that most of us start this Christian journey with a weak faith, afraid that it won't be strong enough to see us through, the Abraham story lets us know that it's not just a weak faith that plagues us as followers of Christ. Ongoing sin plagues us as well. Ongoing sin certainly plagued Abraham's life. I knew Abraham was an idol worshipper when God entered this binding relationship with him. However, what did not register with me before was that Abraham was also a grievous sinner when God bound himself to him. Abraham was a blatant misogynist who treated women, especially his wives, like property that he could dispose of when it benefitted him. He also was a polygamist, which seems to go along with his misogynistic tendencies. On top of this, he had an incestuous marriage. His first or principal wife, Sarah, was also his half-sister. Finally, he did not mind lying to protect himself even when those lies would jeopardize the lives of his wives. Even though I had earlier heard these things in this story, I suppose I somehow downplayed them, wanting Abraham to look more like a good twenty-first century Christian, or at least, to look more acceptable in my contemporary Christian community.

Realizing that I should not downplay the weak faith and grievous sins of Abraham was a big step, especially since God was not trying to hide Abraham's sinfulness from me. Of course, I also realized that the culture Abraham grew up in normalized many of those behaviors such as his incestuous marriage, his polygamy, and to some extent, his misogyny. That doesn't mean those behaviors and practices were right. They certainly were sins. They were what I since have learned to call cultural sins, that is, sins that are so embedded in the fabric of a culture that a person in that culture can't see them as sin and won't be able to see them as sin until the culture itself is significantly changed. But still I wondered, could not God have picked someone a little less flawed to begin His redemptive program? Moreover, if He was going to stick with His choice of someone like Abraham, could He not at least make him give up some of those disgustingly sinful behaviors like the incestuous marriage, the polygamy, and the misogyny? Cultural sins or not, why did God not put His foot down and demand, "Stop it!"

As you know, if you read the story, God never did say stop it. He never did make Abraham give up any of those grievous sins. In fact, at least in the story, God never even brought up those grievous sins with Abraham! Even more shocking is that it was Abraham in the midst of all his ongoing, grievous sinfulness whom God declared righteous, fully accepted, and in a right relationship with Him (Gen. 15:6). It was not Abraham turning from those grievous sins, promising to try to give them up who was declared righteous, but Abraham continuing to live his grievously sinful life who was declared righteous by God. Abraham, with his weak faith, simply trusted God as best he could to keep His promises to him. And it was through that weak faith that Abraham experienced the declaration of being right with God.

God's outrageously graceful commitment to Abraham in this story was hard for me to fathom, and it was hard to fathom because I don't experience this kind of unconditional commitment in any of my earthly relationships. For example, when Abraham grievously sinned against his wife, Sarah, to protect himself, he still was abundantly blessed (Gen. 12:11-20). This challenged my understanding because I had always believed that God could not put up with us in our sinfulness. I thought Abraham should have been severely spanked for treating Sarah the way he did, not graciously blessed. Well, I learned that if I wanted to hang on to my old way of thinking then I would have to stop reading this biblical story too closely. God was not afraid to get his hands dirty with Abraham, Sarah, Isaac,

Jacob, Gideon, Samson, David, Saul, or any of the other grievous sinners in the Old Testament. He doesn't at all seem to be worried about His reputation being sullied by befriending these grievously sinful believers. I might be embarrassed by having someone like Abraham in the church, but that is my problem, not God's. Moreover, it doesn't get any better with the rest of the patriarchal stories. Isaac basically repeated the same kinds of incestuous and misogynistic sins of his father. Jacob doesn't commit the grievous sin of marrying his sister or cousin but does commit an equally grievous sin of marrying two sisters. And if this is too much, then stay away from the story about Jacob's twelve sons, the heads of the twelve tribes of Israel … Reuben the oldest sleeps with his stepmom, Levi and Simeon murder a whole village, and Judah sleeps with his daughter-in-law. And God, while embracing all these grievously sinful descendants of Abraham as his people, won't even begin to address their grievous sins for several centuries, that is until the time of Moses (Leviticus 18). But why did He take so long?

At this point you might be tempted to think that sin doesn't matter all that much to God. That would be a mistake. Of course, sin matters to God. However, as several theologians have noted, the storyteller makes Abraham's sin and unbelief the pivotal point in the story for a reason. Doing so highlights God's grace. Abraham's sin and unfaithfulness are emphasized in this story to show the greatness of God's grace and faithfulness.[3] This is critical to hearing and understanding this story about the beginning of God's redemption program.

It is the very literary structure of this story that draws emphasis to Abraham's sinful, unbelieving practices.[4] God

---

[3] Rachel Yudowsky, "Chaos or Chiasm? The Structure of Abraham's Life", *Jewish Bible Quarterly* 35/2 (2007): 109-114.
[4] Mary Anne Isaak, "Literary Structure and Theology of the Patriarchal Narratives: The Threefold Blessing", *Direction: A*

wants us to know that Abraham was a grievous sinner with a weak faith. It is this grievous sinner with a weak faith whom He called to be the instrument through whom He would begin His plan of reaching all the families of the earth. The first half of the story, which covers a period of ten to fifteen years, emphasizes Abraham's failure to believe God for any of the covenant promises. Each time Abraham responds to one of God's covenant promises with sinful unbelief, God responds to Abraham with grace, staying faithful to him and showering blessings upon him. Then, near the end of the first half of the story, after Abraham's repeated failures to believe God, God again appears to Abraham in a vision just to reassure him of His commitment to His covenant promises (Gen. 15:1-21).

This time when God appears to Abraham to reassure him of his promises, Abraham registers a complaint. This is an interesting moment in the story because most of us would have been too afraid to register a complaint, but not Abraham. He tells God that he wants some stronger assurance than His word that He was going to keep His promise to give him land and descendants! More than ten years had passed since God initially had given His covenant promises and still he, Abraham, had no living descendants. In essence, Abraham was saying, "I know you've promised to give me land and descendants, but now I want you to prove you're going to do it." Surprisingly enough, God, who was revealing himself to Abraham as El Shaddai, the almighty covenant-keeping God, did not get angry. Rather, He calmly responded to Abraham's complaint with one of the most significant events in the Old Testament. He instructed Abram to bring five animals, a heifer, a goat, a ram, a dove, and a pigeon and set up a *"berit,"* a covenant

Mennonite Brethren Forum, Fall 1995, 24/2: 65-74. Rachel Yudowsky, "Chaos or Chiasm? The Structure of Abraham's Life", *Jewish Bible Quarterly* 35/2 (2007): 109-114.

cutting ceremony.[5] This ceremony meant cutting these sacrificed animals in half and placing the halves opposite each other so that a pool of blood formed between them. Both covenant participants would then walk through the pool of blood between the animal parts as a way of saying, "May what was done to these animals be done to me if I do not keep my part of this covenant agreement."[6]

Abram set up the covenant cutting ceremony and then the unexpected, the extraordinary happened. God alone passed through the pool of blood between the animal parts. El Shaddai, the almighty, covenant-keeping God, alone took all of the responsibilities and burdens for keeping the covenant relationship. He of course assumed responsibility for His part of the covenant relationship, but He also assumed responsibility for Abraham's part in the covenant relationship. First, He passed through as a smoking firepot and then He passed through as a flaming torch.[4] This had to be unbelievable for Abraham. By going alone God, as *El Shaddai*, was declaring that He alone was responsible for keeping the covenant. By passing through the blood and animal parts as the smoking pot and as the flaming torch, He was invoking the curse upon Himself if either He or Abram failed to keep their covenant commitments.[7] With incredible grace, ***God, as El Shaddai, was declaring that the fulfillment of the covenant promises solely depended on Him and His faithfulness not Abraham's.***

Up to this point in the story, Abraham had not lived up to his part in the covenant relationship. Every time God

---

[5] Christopher T. Begg, "The Covenantal Dove in Psalm 74:19-20", *Veyus Testamentum 37* (January 1988): 79. This was a common way to ratify a covenant in the Ancient Near East, so common in fact that God did not have to tell Abram how to set up the ceremony. Moreover, it was such common knowledge that the ancient Hebrew listeners would have clearly understood its meaning as well.

[6] John Mark Hicks, *Come to the Table* (Orange, CA: New Leaf Books, 2002), 28.

[7] Ibid., 29.

tested him to see if he would trust Him to keep His promises, Abraham responded in sinful unbelief. He had abandoned the promised land after God had appeared to him and told him he was in the land on which his descendants would be raised up. He fled to Egypt where he continued to act in sinful unbelief, lying about Sarah being his wife to protect himself, even if it meant harm to Sarah. This act showed that Abraham had given up on both the covenant promise of protection and the covenant promise of descendants. But now, now that God had done the incredible, overwhelmed him with grace in the covenant cutting ceremony, how would he, Abraham, respond? That is when we arrive at the center of the story, that is, the focal point of this story. Will Abraham finally start responding to God with faithful obedience? Unfortunately, the answer is no. Even though God had touched Abraham with incredible grace through the covenant cutting ceremony, Abraham continued to respond to God in sinful unbelief. The central focus of the story occurs after the covenant cutting ceremony when Abraham, instead of trusting God to keep His promise of giving him descendants, acted in unbelief by taking Sarah's maid Hagar as a concubine and producing a child born of his unbelief, Ishmael (Gen. 16).

We tend to be surprised that this is the central focus of the Abraham story. We should not be. The storyteller is driving the point home that God as *El Shaddai* takes on full responsibility for keeping the covenant relationship because only God can keep the covenant relationship with us. This covenant relationship with all of its promises was 100 percent dependent on God, as *El Shaddai*, the almighty covenant-keeping God. To know and worship God as *El Shaddai* is to know and worship the God who is powerful enough to keep the covenant relationship with us not because we are faithful and obedient to Him, but because He is faithful to us. This focus in the Abraham story is so important that it is repeated in the Isaac/Jacob story (Gen.

25-37) and in the story of the twelve sons of Jacob (Gen. 38-50).

The second half of the Abraham story is just as surprising and just as beautiful as the first half. The second half begins thirteen years later with God responding to Abraham's great act of unbelief with GRACE ... God as *El Shaddai* returns to Abraham and reiterates His covenant promises to him. He also reminds him that he was to live a blameless life before God, something Abraham has obviously failed to do. And then the extraordinary happens. God gives Abraham the covenant sign, circumcision. This covenant sign was not to remind God that Abraham belonged to Him. Rather, it was to remind Abraham that he and his descendants belonged to God. From this point on, Abraham and his descendants would bear a physical sign on their bodies that they belonged to El Shaddai, the almighty covenant-keeping God.

While Abraham has learned much by this point in his relationship with God, he is still learning what it means to trust God to keep his promises. That is why in the midst of having God as *El Shaddai* reiterate His covenant promise, give him the covenant sign, and change his name from Abram (exalted father) to Abraham (father of a multitude of nations), the storyteller states that Abraham continued to haggle with God about letting Ishmael, the child born of his unbelief, be the promised covenant heir. *El Shaddai* would have no part in it. Even later when Sarah laughs in unbelief about God keeping His promise to give them a son, God acts surprised that this couple is still having a hard time believing in him (Gen. 18:1-13). However, to strengthen their weak faith, God tells them that once the promised heir is born, they are to name him Isaac, which means laughter, simply to remind them that they laughed in unbelief at the promise-keeping God.

By now we should be getting the flow of this story. The storyteller has repeatedly reminded us that Abraham is unable to fulfill his responsibilities in the covenant relationship. Repeatedly, he failed to trust God for any of His covenant promises. And repeatedly, God responded to him with grace. But we are going to be reminded one more time. This event occurred shortly after God appeared to Abraham to reiterate His covenant promises, give him the covenant sign, change his name, and promise that Sarah would give birth to their long-awaited descendant within the next year. Abraham and Sarah moved to a different part of Canaan where Abraham was encountered by a potentate named Abimelech. It would not be long before Sarah would conceive and be in the early stages of her pregnancy. It didn't matter, because for whatever reason, Abraham again feared for his life and, to protect himself, lied about Sarah being his wife. The king thus took Sarah and once again, because of Abraham's sinful unbelief, both God's promise of protection and His promise of Abraham and Sarah's long-awaited descendant were threatened. Of course, God again graciously responded and rescued Sarah, and she was reunited with Abraham (Gen. 20:1-18).

This has been a beautiful story about God's grace. God gave Abraham promises that when fulfilled, would allow Abraham and his descendants to be a blessing to all the world. He then tested Abraham. The test is not simply to see if Abraham would trust God to keep His promises, but to see if Abraham could trust God to keep His promises. And the answer to both questions is no! Abraham was asked to trust God for every one of the covenant promises He had given, and in every situation in which Abraham was asked to believe God for a specific promise, he failed to trust and obey God for that promise. And each time Abraham failed to believe and obey, God responded with grace, keeping the covenant promises to him in spite of Abraham's unbelief and disobedience. This story does not just define grace, it allows us to experience God's grace in the life of Abraham. This is the reason, so many centuries later, the Apostle Paul would use this story to illustrate what God's grace was like to the churches in Galatia and Rome. But the story is not yet over. Up to this point, we have seen that grace allows Abraham to experience the declaration of being right with God. The experience of God's grace, however, does more than get us declared right with God. The experience of grace also changes us and that is what we see in the last part of the Abraham story.

In this last part of the story, God tested Abraham one more time. This test comes more than forty years after God had first called Abraham into a unique relationship. In that unique relationship, Abraham continued to struggle with doubt, unbelief, and disobedience while God graciously, patiently, and lovingly engraved *"Trust Me"* into his heart. Now, forty years later, God would again ask Abraham to trust Him, and this time, He would ask him to trust Him to keep His promise about Isaac being the covenant heir through whom God would continue fulfilling His covenant promises (Gen. 17:19). So, He told Abraham to go to Mt. Moriah and offer up Isaac as a sacrifice. By the time Abraham arrived at Mt. Moriah, we, along with Abraham can look back over his life and see, time and again, more than forty years of God's gracious faithfulness, His unmerited and unconditional love for one who often stumbled. But this time, Abraham did not stumble. This time Abraham believed. After forty years, Abraham was sure of the fact that El Shaddai could be trusted. In fact, this time Abraham believed so much that *El Shaddai*, the covenant-keeping God, would keep His promise concerning Isaac that he told the servants accompanying him on the journey to Mt. Moriah that he and Isaac would both be coming back down the mountain after the sacrifice was made (Gen. 22:5). And he believed so much that *El Shaddai* would keep his promise concerning Isaac that he even told Isaac that God himself would provide the lamb for the sacrifice when Isaac asked him about it (Gen. 22:8).

And as the writer of the book of Hebrews informs us, Abraham believed so much that God would keep His covenant promise concerning Isaac that even if God had to raise Isaac from the dead, the two of them would come down from the mountain (Hebrews 11:17-19). Finally, Abraham believed that God would keep His promises, and that is when God himself rejoiced (22:15-18). God's grace did so much more than declare Abraham to be righteous (which in itself is plenty to rejoice about). Abraham's experience of God's grace also built faith and obedience into his life. For Abraham, faith and obedience were not things he offered to God to earn His blessing; they were the things of which God, through His marvelous grace, blessed his life.

So, now I will return to the issue that I began addressing. How has entering this part of God's story challenged and changed me regarding the issue of ongoing sin in the Church? First, entering this part of God's story allows me to embrace the grievous sinner Abraham the same way God embraces him, with grace. If God graciously embraces and befriends a grievously sinful believer such as Abraham with his polygamous, incestuous marriage, then I should as well. But, not just Abraham, I should also graciously embrace and befriend the Nahuatl believers with their polygamous marriages whom I spoke about earlier. I should also recognize that grievous sinners might not see their ongoing sin as sin. I could try confronting these sinners with their sin, but if they don't see it as sin, and especially if it is a cultural sin, then confrontation probably won't work. So, like God did with Abraham, I should continue to graciously embrace and befriend these believers even if I think they are living in ongoing sin. Moreover, I should expect other believers to recognize that I too might be blind to my own grievous sin and should expect them to graciously embrace and befriend me. They should confront me, but also remember that it is God's job to convict me of my sin.

Finally, I should continue in prayer. I should pray, asking God for greater clarity both for myself and for the other person. Conviction of sin is part of God's ongoing work in His church and I should be patient as God faithfully does His work.

Radically Following Jesus in a Fallen World
– Brandon Miller

Recall

"Islamic State Video Shows Beheadings of Egyptian Christians in Libya."[1] This was the headline of a New York Times article published on Monday, February 15, 2015, referring to a video—which was allegedly released the day before—by an ISIS-affiliated organization. On that day, various print and televised news reports flooded media outlets as the facts of this horrific ordeal were painted in graphic detail.

Twenty-one Coptic Christians clad in orange jumpsuits, were marched down a rocky beach off the coast of the Mediterranean Sea, with their hands restrained behind their backs. The twenty-one Christian men were escorted by masked fighters dressed in all black "identified as from the Tripolitania Province of the Islamic State."[2] Lined up at the water's edge, the hostages were forced to kneel in the sand as their captors stood behind them with blades in hand. After several moments of threatening propaganda, the attackers pushed the Egyptians forward and began their bloody executions.

---

[1] Kirkpatrick, David D. And Rukmini Callimachi. *"Islamic State Video Shows Beheadings of Egyptian Christians in Libya."* The New York Times, 15 Feb. 2015.

[2] Ibid.

Unfortunately, in recent times, this terrifying story is not an isolated event. Threats and demonstrations of similar types of attacks are commonplace in our everyday news reporting.

Open Doors, a nonprofit organization focused on serving persecuted Christians worldwide, posted the following on its website: "Each month 322 Christians are killed for their faith, 214 churches and Christian properties are destroyed, and 772 forms of violence are committed against Christians (such as … abductions, rape, arrests and forced marriages)." They went on to say,

> From verbal harassment to hostile feelings, attitudes, and actions, Christians in areas with severe religious restrictions pay a heavy price for their faith. Beatings, physical torture, confinement, isolation … severe punishment, imprisonment, slavery, discrimination in education and employment, and even death are just a few examples of the persecution they experience on a daily basis.[3]

As we recall the videos and images of the blood from the twenty-one Egyptian Christians intermingled with the waves crashing on the Mediterranean shore, we cannot help but call our own safety and security into serious question, even as followers of an all-powerful God.

Rewind

If we could rewind the Christian historical timeline, we would call to mind countless other stories of persecution for nearly two millennia since the time of Christ. Literature and movies such as *Tortured for Christ, End of the Spear, Jesus Freaks, Foxe's Book of Martyrs, The Heavenly Man, The Insanity of God,*

---

[3] *"Christian Persecution."* Open Doors USA, www.opendoorsusa.org/christian-persecution/.

and so many others recount a plethora of precious stories depicting various victimized saints throughout the ages.

In what is often referred to as the Bible's "Hall of Faith," the writer of Hebrews describes various inspiring stories of Biblical men and women, who did many great and mighty works for God by faith. Hebrews 11:35, however, takes a sobering turn in the chapter. The author of Hebrews writes:

> [35] ... But others were tortured, refusing to turn from God in order to be set free. They placed their hope in a better life after the resurrection. [36] Some were jeered at, and their backs were cut open with whips. Others were chained in prisons. [37] Some died by stoning, some were sawed in half, and others were killed with the sword. Some went about wearing skins of sheep and goats, destitute and oppressed and mistreated. [38]... wandering over deserts and mountains, hiding in caves and holes in the ground.

Although we have a dangerous tendency to take their stories for granted, we ought to realize we are eternally indebted to the incredible sacrifices these men and women endured in order that we might have access to the life-giving truth of the gospel of Jesus Christ. Let us never cease to reflect on the horrendous prices paid by the saints throughout the ages.

Review

A review of Biblical accounts of persecution will not let us ignore the ways the early apostles died. Although the Bible makes little mention of the end of their lives, National

Geographic released an article, outlining supposed ways the Apostles of Christ died from various sources:

> Simon-Peter … asked to be crucified upside down, so that his death would not be the equal of Jesus … Andrew was scourged, and then tied rather than nailed to a cross, so that he would suffer for a longer time before dying. Andrew lived for two days, during which he preached to passersby … James was killed with a sword … John was the only one of the original disciples not to die a violent death. Instead, he passed away peacefully in Patmos… Philip … was scourged, thrown into prison, and crucified … In one account, 'impatient idolaters' beat Bartholomew and then crucified him, while in another, he was skinned alive and then beheaded … Thomas … angered local religious authorities, who martyred him by running him through with a spear … Matt. … was supposedly stabbed in the back by a swordsman … James … was beaten and stoned by persecutors, and then killed him by hitting him in the head with a club … Jude: was crucified … Simon the Zealot was crucified…

In light of the courage the Apostles displayed, we cannot afford to overlook the fact that many of these men were the same ones who—at one point or another—doubted, denied, discredited, and even abandoned Jesus while he was on earth. So, what changed to cause these men to bravely face opposition, and even death, for the sake of the gospel? I'm convinced they had an eyewitness encounter with the risen Christ.

Reflect

One such man, who had a firsthand encounter with Christ, was the Apostle Paul. Paul had a life-altering experience with the Lord on the road to Damascus. This experience changed Paul's life and made him the great man of faith we know and study today.

In his second letter to the Corinthians, we see him reflect on his sufferings for the sake of Christ. In chapter eleven, verses 23-28 we see that Paul was no stranger to suffering.

> 23 …in labours more abundant, in stripes above measure, in prisons more frequent, in deaths oft. 24 Of the Jews five times received I forty stripes save one. 25 Thrice was I beaten with rods, once was I stoned, thrice I suffered shipwreck, a night and a day I have been in the deep; 26 In journeyings often, in perils of waters, in perils of robbers, in perils by mine own countrymen, in perils by the heathen, in perils in the city, in perils in the wilderness, in perils in the sea, in perils among false brethren; 27 In weariness and painfulness, in watchings often, in hunger and thirst, in fastings often, in cold and nakedness. 28 Beside those things that are without, that which cometh upon me daily, the care of all the churches.

We must not forget that this man, the highly revered Apostle Paul of Second Corinthians, was formerly known as Saul of Tarsus. Saul led an aggressive charge to persecute early Christians. In Acts 8, Saul is giving consent to the death-by-stoning of the first Christian martyr, Stephen. After Stephen's death, Saul wreaked havoc on the church, entering into houses and dragging both men and women off to prison. Acts 9 says that Saul was "uttering threats with every breath and was eager to kill the Lord's followers." This onslaught would scatter the early church abroad and would unintentionally prove to be one of the most significant evangelistic events in Christian history.

Remember

Our final flashback takes us to a man the locals called Yeshua. Several years after his cousin, John the Baptist, had his head delivered on a platter at a birthday party, Jesus of Nazareth spent several years healing the sick, raising the dead, feeding multitudes, and meeting the needs of the poor, outcasts, and less fortunate. The citizens thanked him with a blindfold as they spat upon, struck with fists, scourged with a cat of nine tails, stripped, and mocked this innocent man.

The carpenter's son was later struck with the same rod that Roman soldiers used earlier to press a crown of thorns down on his already bruised head. This fellow Jew, born in Bethlehem, was led down the Via Dolorosa carrying a heavy cross beam on his back. With some wails of horror and other shouts of scorn, the crowd watched as Jesus was taken to Golgotha, the Place of the Skull.

Roman soldiers stretched his broken body across the wooden cross and hammered nails into both of his calloused hands. A final nail was driven through the flesh, tendons, and bony feet of the One the prophet Isaiah wrote about some 700 years before.[4] The soldiers gambled for

---

[4] "*Bible prophecies fulfilled: Bible prophecies that found fulfillment during the life of Jesus Christ.*" 100prophecies.org, www.100prophecies.org/page3.htm.

Jesus' clothes and minutes before he breathed his last, The King of the Jews cried out, "Father, forgive them, for they know not what they do."[5]

Fast Forward

As we recall, rewind, review, reflect, and remember the stories of Christians taking up their cross to follow Jesus (Matthew 16: 24-26) for the last two thousand years, let us fast forward to our modern-day version of Christianity in America. Each Sunday, we drive millions of dollars' worth of cars, park outside of millions of dollars' worth of buildings, and sit contentedly inside our well-lit, perfectly air-conditioned sanctuaries.

We hear sermons that will often sound like nothing more than a fluffy pep talk. We coin incorrect catch phrases like: "Name It and Claim It" or "Blab It and Grab It," all while submitting ourselves to the positive confessions of a "health and wealth doctrine" that looks nothing like what Jesus promised. We believe whatever wind of doctrine comes our way, even if in its self-centered claims make erroneous boasts such as God just wants you to be happy, rich, comfortable, safe, or any number of other things that cannot be founded on the full counsel of scripture. Just ask Jesus into your heart, we hear. You just need to say a prayer, we believe. Do this, and you can go on living the American dream version of Christianity that has plagued our culture for decades.

For the majority of Western Christians, persecution looks much different than it did in the stories we previously examined. Many who profess to be Christians won't share their faith because they are afraid that someone might disagree with them. As a result, far too many so-called Christians will not stand up for holy, honorable, and life-

---

[5] Luke 23:34, King James Version.

giving truth, whenever and wherever there's a risk of being labeled narrow-minded or politically incorrect.

In the United States, we've somehow stooped to believing that even in following Christ, our carnal lives won't have to change very much. But how can we read passages like Luke 9:23-26, Luke 9:57-62, Luke 14:25-35, or so many others, and not realize that the safe, comfortable, Americanized version of Christianity that we experience, sounds nothing like what Jesus himself established? These passages speak of costly self-denial, unashamed abandonment, and intentional sacrifice, but challenges to live with this type of upward calling are scarce in American pulpits. While we "play church" in the U.S., I can almost hear Jesus—bloody upon the cross—echoing words along with the saints from nearly two millennia of persecution, saying, "Father, forgive them for they know not what they do."

Counting the Cost

The purpose of my comment is not to dissuade anyone from starting a relationship with Jesus Christ, nor is it my intention to universalize the beliefs and actions of any religious establishment. There is, however, wisdom in considering what could be, or perhaps should be, at stake when making such a life-altering decision as radically following Jesus.

In Luke 14:28, Jesus begins encouraging the multitude to count the cost of following Him. Throughout scripture, we see that on this side of heaven, we cannot expect a world without pain, loss, tears, hostility, or even death. Although there is a blessed hope as an anchor for the believer's soul and an ever-present help in times of trouble, Jesus never promised a life free of trials. On the contrary, Jesus taught things like, "Behold, I send you out as sheep in the midst of wolves," and "You will be hated by all for My name's sake."[6]

John 16:33 unpacks a plain, yet often ignored, truth from Christ. Jesus clearly communicates, "...in this world you will have trouble..." Christians do the world a severe disservice if they inaccurately promise or imply that following Jesus means life on Earth will be a bed of roses. I learned this firsthand on December 17, 2005.

Following Jesus Through Tragedy

A week before Christmas Eve of my senior year in high school my family went through the most untimely and grievous tragedy of our lives. I am privileged to be a part of an amazing and loving family. Both of my parents have faithfully served Christ my entire life, and I am extremely grateful to God for such exceptional Christian role models.

I made a personal decision to become a disciple and follower of Christ when I was young and consistently strived to follow Him throughout my adolescence. My brother, Chad Edward Miller, was born when I was five years old. Although we fought and bickered like brothers do, I had an inexpressible relationship with Chad. We were five years apart, yet we did everything together. Saturday, December 17, 2005, was no exception.

We spent the morning at a church-sponsored outreach in our community. After the event, we met my parents at our family-owned apartment complex, where we worked with them to prepare a unit for rent. Around dusk, we decided it was going to be family movie night. The plan was for Chad and I to stop by the video store to grab the film. My parents would clean up and meet us at home for an evening full of family fun.

Unfortunately, we never made it to the video store that night. I fell asleep at the wheel. We drifted off the road,

---

[6] Matthew 10:16-22, New King James Version.

crashing into a tree. Despite valiant efforts by first responders, care flight personnel, and hospital staff, Chad—who was riding in my passenger seat—went to be with the Lord.

In the face of such a horrifying tragedy, it is common to hear and to ask, "Why me God? Why did you let this or that happen?" Or one might ask it this way: "Why do bad things happen to good people?" I wish I could say that I had the faith to refrain from these thoughts, feelings, and questions, but the truth is, I went through a prolonged period where I was pondering these exact questions. Yet, I can honestly testify that—although I would not want to experience the depths of this loss again—it wasn't until I went through this fiery trial, that my faith truly became rooted and grounded in the all-surpassing greatness of God. It was through the death of my brother that I began to see what radically following Jesus really looks like.

I found that suffering is the product of a fallen world, but I also discovered that God uses suffering as a purposeful platform to reveal and display His unconditional, selfless, and sacrificial love for fallen humanity. Through the darkest times of my life, I have found that there is—in fact—purpose in whatever pain, problem, or persecution we experience in this sin-cursed world.

Why Me?

The "why me" question is one that cannot be quickly answered within the confines of this chapter. Simply put, however, I want to encourage you that in the midst of these trying tribulations, you can have confidence that God is with you!

Can I offer you the hope that, through Christ, the "why me" questions of life and all the emotions behind these questions can actually begin to fade away slowly as we surrender to the love of God? Our deepest concerns can be resolved, and we can start to joyfully endure the trials of life, if we could just learn to rephrase the "why me" question.

What would happen if, instead of asking "why me," we started to ask God, "why YOU?" God, why would YOU choose to suffer? Why would YOU, who knew no sin, choose to become sin for me? God why would YOU step down into my sin-cursed situation and not just suffer for me on a cross, but suffer with me in my afflictions?

Reflect on that for a moment. There is surely a reason, surely a plan, and surely a purpose that God not only suffered for us, but suffers with us. Hebrews 4:14-16 says:

> [14] Seeing then that we have a great high priest, that is passed into the heavens, Jesus the Son of God, let us hold fast our profession. [15] For we have not a high priest which cannot be touched with the feeling of our infirmities; but was in all points tempted like as we are, yet without sin. [16] Let us therefore come boldly unto the throne of grace, that we may obtain mercy, and find grace to help in time of need.

R.C. Sproul once said, "Why do bad things happen to good people? That only happened once, and he volunteered."[7] The answer to the question, "why do bad things happen to good people" is profoundly simple: Through the sacrificial love of the only true good person, Jesus Christ, we find that the primary purpose of his suffering was simply to be with us. Jesus loves us so much that he longs to be with us while we're on this sin cursed earth, and to be with us for all eternity in heaven. Therefore,

---

[7] Sproul Jr, R.C. "R.C. Sproul Jr. Quotes." GoodReads.com, https://www.goodreads.com/author/quotes/227508.R_C_Sproul_Jr_.

I believe, one of the primary purposes for our suffering is to be with Him. To be with Him on this sin cursed earth, and to be with Him for eternity in heaven!

Blessed Reward

Chapter five of Matthew's gospel boldly proclaims a truth that is hard to agree with, without a proper understanding of God's purposes for allowing suffering. Matthew records Jesus saying:

> [10] Blessed are they which are persecuted for righteousness' sake: for theirs is the kingdom of heaven. [11] Blessed are ye, when men shall revile you, and persecute you, and shall say all manner of evil against you falsely, for my sake. [12] Rejoice, and be exceeding glad: for great is your reward in heaven …

These verses reveal a secret concerning how believers are able to endure various hardships in life. True followers of Jesus experience a radical transformation and renewal of mind. Genuine disciples of Christ no longer live with earthly prerogative; but they thrive with an eternal perspective. When keeping in mind the eternal glory awaiting us, we begin to realize that Christ endured suffering to offer—and we can endure suffering to enjoy—a future inheritance to which nothing in this world can compare. This is why Paul could write 2 Corinthians 4, and in light of all he went through, could say:

> [17] For our light affliction, which is but for a moment, worketh for us a far more exceeding and eternal weight of glory; [18] While we look not at the things which

are seen, but at the things which are not
seen: for the things which are seen are
temporal; but the things which are not
seen are eternal.

Commenting on our spiritual adoption into the family of
God he says in Romans 8:

> 17 ... if so be that we suffer with him, that
> we may be also glorified together. 18 For I
> reckon that the sufferings of this present
> time are not worthy to be compared with
> the glory which shall be revealed in us.

> Paul goes on to remind us that no matter
> what we face, "28 ... we know that all
> things work together for good to them that
> love God, to them who are called
> according to his purpose."

Even at the end of Paul's life, he shared the following
thoughts to young Timothy in 1 Timothy 4:

> 5 But watch thou in all things, endure
> afflictions, do the work of an evangelist,
> make full proof of thy ministry... 7 I have
> fought a good fight, I have finished my
> course, I have kept the faith: 8 Henceforth
> there is laid up for me a crown of
> righteousness, which the Lord, the
> righteous judge, shall give me at that day:
> and not to me only, but unto all them also
> that love his appearing.

Paul certainly had an eternal perspective in the midst of his fiery trials. My encouragement for every believer and non-believer alike, is to study these passages and others like them, while praying that God would give us proper spiritual perception as we endeavor to see what it truly means to follow Jesus in a fallen world.

Radically Following Jesus in A Sin-Cursed World

With these truths in view, let us conclude by considering what it might look like to radically follow Jesus through the sufferings of a sin-cursed world. Radical faith in Jesus Christ is counting the cost, daily taking up your cross, and following Him wherever that leads (even if it means trusting Christ in the midst of suffering, pain, tragedy, or persecution). From personal experience, the testimony of the saints throughout the ages, and the authority of God's word, I am confident—in the midst of opposition, maltreatment, trials, calamities, and tribulations—a life abandoned to the Lordship of Jesus Christ is the most incredible, fulfilling, and REWARDING adventure imaginable, both here and for eternity! Why? Because Yeshua, the author and finisher of our faith, said "Lo, **I am with you always**, even unto the end of the world!"[8]

---

[8] Matthew 28:20, King James Version.

Finding the Greatest Treasure
– Kevin Rusack

I met Jesus in my dorm room at the age of eighteen. That statement is a bit weird because I was raised in a churchgoing home and heard stories about Jesus my whole life. Our family attended services every Sunday, so I was exposed to a wide variety of religious experiences—Sunday School, retreats, hymns, etc. I even sang in the church choir. If you had asked me I would have said I believed in God, but as I moved into my teen years it became evident that I wasn't a follower of God, but rather a devoted follower of the hook up and party culture of my day. If you would have analyzed my life choices when I left home at the age of seventeen, you would have easily concluded that my religion of choice was hedonism. If it felt good, I wanted to experience it. Thoughts of church and Jesus were discarded and replaced with a drive for success and self-fulfillment. Everything seemed to be going just fine until I met my new roommate, Dave.

I knew I was in big trouble the day I moved into my new dorm and saw the huge Bible sitting on the desk by his bed. I thought, "Oh great! I get to live with a religious nut job!" And I came to find out that Dave was truly nuts about Jesus. He went to church three times a week. Who does that?! To make matters worse, he listened to Christian music and had frequent Bible studies in our room. But the thing that really mystified me was how Dave treated me. He was nice. Really nice. And what I couldn't wrap my head around was the fact that he seemed to really care about me—and I was a jerk of a roommate! Instead of condemning my sins, Dave simply did the best he could to introduce me to Jesus. Slowly, over time, I became convinced that he had something that I didn't have. His Christian life became so attractive to me that I started visiting churches, and I heard the gospel. Within six months of meeting Dave, I prayed on my knees in our dorm room and gave my heart to Jesus.

Right away, I noticed that something was different from my churchgoing experience as a kid. This time, I actually intended to follow and obey God. There was an allegiance change. At a core level, I understood that I was no longer in charge of my life. I was accepting Jesus, not just as a religious figure to admire, but as Lord of my life, One who I would live for and obey. I didn't know it at the time, but my heart attitude aligned with what Jesus said in Luke 9:23: "If anyone would come after me, he must deny himself and take up his cross daily and follow me. For whoever wants to save his life will lose it, but whoever loses his life for me will save it."

I have to say that the first year of learning to walk with Jesus was euphoric. I experienced a new joy that was uncontainable, a love for people—even difficult ones, and an ability to say no to unhealthy habits I had indulged in previously. I came to understand that this is what the Holy Spirit does when He comes to reside in a human heart; the changes were all a part of becoming a "new creation" as described by the Apostle Paul in 2 Corinthians 5:17. In the next few years, there were numerous experiences and truths that I came to understand that radically impacted my spiritual life and they became a foundation that I still build upon today.

One of these truths that began to crystallize early on was that my view of God impacted everything. Growing up, I had envisioned God as a distant and rather grouchy deity who had made up a bunch of rules that seemed designed to suck all the fun out of life. But as I read my Bible, a different picture began to materialize. My eyes were opened to a God who was approachable; a heavenly Father who said things like, "Come near to God, and He will come near to you" (James 4:8). It seemed that the Creator wasn't far away on the back side of Alpha Centauri watching us on a big screen TV after all! Rather, He was near and present and ready to make Himself known to those who would take the time to seek Him.

My perspective became even clearer when I read the words of Jesus in John 17:3, "Now this is eternal life: that they may *know you*, the only true God, and Jesus Christ whom you have sent." So according to Jesus, the goal of eternal life is what? It is to know God. Understanding this truth helped me to see that the primary goal of Christianity is not to gain enough doctrinal facts about sin and salvation to secure a home in heaven. Eternal life is an incredible invitation to get to know the most exciting personality in the universe for all of time.

Sadly, however, I have met many churchgoers over the years who live with the view that eternal life is only about the forgiveness of their sins. It is about being pardoned, praise God, but it is also so much more. A person who lives with this limited view of salvation is like a person who suddenly inherits a castle or mansion and chooses to live in the entrance hall the rest of their life, never experiencing life in the rest of the house. That would be crazy!

When I began to realize that Jesus stepped into time and came to earth to remove all the barriers holding me back from fully relating to Him, and that He actually *wanted* me to know Him, the result was a newfound desire that propelled me toward a passionate pursuit of knowing God.

As an understanding of God began to take root in my heart, some very timely and providential things occurred. The first was I read A.W. Tozer's book "The Pursuit of God." Tozer was a pastor and theologian of the twentieth century considered by many in the church to be a modern-day prophet. He challenged the status quo. His words challenged me to question my spiritual depth and experience of God, and expanded my paradigm of the Creator. He wrote: "We have almost forgotten that God is a person and, as such, can be cultivated as any person can." He went on to say:

> Religion, so far as it is genuine, is in essence the response of created personalities to the creating personality, God. He is a person, and in the deep of His mighty nature He thinks, wills, enjoys, feels, loves, desires, and suffers as any other person may. In making Himself known to us He stays by the familiar pattern of personality. He communicates with us through the avenues of our minds, our wills, and our emotions.[1]

As I read these words they confirmed what I had been seeing in my Bible and feeling in my heart—that God is indeed knowable on an intimate level, and the primary purpose of my life on this earth is to get to know Him!

After looking at seminaries and theology programs to further my pursuit of knowing God, I ultimately decided to take a season to gain experience in doing the things that Jesus did—preaching the gospel and caring for the poor. I figured that one of the best ways to get to know someone is to work on a project with them. My search for an organization that would train me and send me to the nations led me to Youth with a Mission (YWAM). When I learned that their motto was "To know God and to make Him known," I knew I was headed in the right direction.

---

[1] Tozer, A. W. *The Pursuit of God.* Camp Hill, PA: Christian Publications, 1982.

In the months of training that followed, another truth became clear: Salvation is a free gift, but intimacy requires effort. This is true in any relationship. For example, when I started to get to know my wife, I knew some facts about her early on. If you had asked me during our first year of dating I would have said that I knew her. But after being married for several years, traveling the world, and raising three kids together, I would say that I'm really getting to know her. I'm learning how she's wired; what she loves and what fires her up; I better understand her hopes, fears, and dreams. That type of knowing has required many hours of back-and-forth dialogue and interaction. Intimacy requires effort.

When it comes to knowing God, it can be a bit confusing to understand how much of the relationship depends on Him and how much of it depends on us. Exactly how much effort is required on our part? Why doesn't God just show up in a burning bush like he did with Moses? That would make things much easier, right? The answer is that there is a dynamic tension between our pursuit of God and His pursuit of us. This tension is described in Philippians 2:12-13, which reads, "Work out your salvation with fear and trembling; for it is God who is at work in you, both to will and to work for His good pleasure."

We see in the scriptures that God works to draw us to Himself, and He initiates the work of grace in our hearts, but the outworking of that is our following hard after Him. A.W. Tozer reminds us that "all the time we are pursuing Him we are already in His hand."[2]

The Bible also makes it clear that *how* you and I pursue God seems to determine what we will experience. He says, "You will seek me and find me when you seek me with all your heart" (Jer. 29:13). This means that the way we pursue God matters. We must put our heart into it. Most of us understand the idea of passionate pursuit when it comes to

---

[2] Ibid.

things like the boy or girl we want to date, getting into the school we really want to attend, or landing our dream job. What we value drives our actions. The same energy that motivates us toward what we value in life applies to the way we seek after God.

When I was a kid, treasure hunts intrigued me. I would daydream about discovering some old map in the attic that would lead to a lost treasure. My two boys share that same fascination. I recently observed them burying a box full of their allowance money under our trampoline! Popular movies such as The Goonies, National Treasure, Indiana Jones, and The Count of Monte Cristo show that people want to discover treasure, and they will go to just about any length to do so.

When I was probably ten or eleven, my twin brother and I decided one summer day to dig a hole in our friend Brian's backyard. We wanted to see just how deep we could dig. It made perfect sense, so the three of us started to dig in the hot sun. The progress was slow. Finally, we started to see a black substance mixed in with the dirt. We all turned towards each other with our mouths hanging open as it hit us—we had discovered oil! Visions of all the toys I could buy with my new wealth filled my head. I could get that new bike! We started to dig faster and faster. We forgot about our tiredness and sore muscles. We put our hearts into digging because we had discovered a treasure. After a little while we dispatched Brian to run in and tell his dad about our newly found fortune. When his dad heard the news, he smiled, shook his head, and said, "You boys go fill that hole back in. You just uncovered the spot where I dumped the old oil from my car." I guess we weren't going to be rich after all! That's a funny story, but you see, there's just something about treasure that causes people to expend more energy, more time, more of anything else in their life to find it, to search for it, and to find it. Value prompts action.

King Solomon, the wisest man to walk the earth before Jesus came along, spoke directly to this idea of searching for treasure and the way we come to know God:

> If you call out for insight
> and cry aloud for understanding,
> ⁴ and if you look for it as for silver
> and **search for it as for hidden treasure**,
> ⁵ then you will understand the fear of the Lord
> and **find the knowledge of God**. (Prov. 2:3-5)

Jesus gave us two parables about this value and pursuit paradigm.

> ⁴⁴The kingdom of heaven is like treasure hidden in a field. When a man found it, he hid it again, and then in his joy went and sold all he had and bought that field. ⁴⁵ Again, the kingdom of heaven is like a merchant looking for fine pearls. ⁴⁶ When he found one of great value, he went away and sold everything he had and bought it (Matt. 13:44-45).

These two parables depict two kinds of pursuers. The first one is a seeker who is surprised by what he finds. He's not really looking and just stumbles across the treasure (like we did when we uncovered a hidden oil deposit in the backyard). This kind of seeker describes me when I came to know Jesus. I wasn't really looking for God at the time. He swept into my life by surprise. Looking back on it, God was probably moving in my life, due in part to the prayers of my roommate and my godly grandmothers.

On the other hand, the second parable Jesus told describes a determined seeker who finally finds that thing that he is looking for. He is not a casual seeker. He has a plan of pursuit.

When I think about someone coming to faith in this fashion I think about Rosaria Butterfield. She was a former tenured professor at the University of Syracuse. Rosaria was also a radical feminist and an atheist. Now she's a pastor's wife and a powerful Christian writer and speaker. She says that one of the biggest things God used to cultivate her heart to believe in Jesus was her interaction with a local pastor named Ken Smith. He first wrote her a kind, inquiring letter about an article she had written. She says the letter really messed with her presuppositions and worldview and made her curious about why Ken believed what he did about Jesus. Like the pearl merchant in Jesus' parable, Rosaria decided to go on a search. When Ken invited Rosaria to his house to discuss his beliefs more fully, she accepted. She thought it would be good "research." But something more than the collecting of information occurred—Ken and his wife, Floy, became Rosaria's friends. They entered her world, and they met her friends. They did book exchanges. When they ate together, Ken prayed in a way she had never heard before. As the relationship grew she started meeting with them regularly to read the Bible together. Slowly, over time the Bible began to take on a meaning that startled this atheist English professor, and two years from the time she started reading the Bible, she trusted in Jesus as her savior. Her search led to the find of a lifetime.[3]

As we start out on our quest for the greatest treasure of all, we must not be naïve. Think back to all the "Indiana Jones" type movies you watched growing up. What usually surrounded the treasure in each of the movies? Booby traps. One of the biggest booby traps that stops us in our pursuit of knowing God is that we give up too soon. We settle into a mindset that says, "I'm just not feeling anything, and I don't seem to be changing fast enough. Maybe God isn't

---

[3] Butterfield, Rosaria Champagne. *The Secret Thoughts of an Unlikely Convert: An English Professor's Journey into Christian Faith*. Pittsburgh, PA: Crown & Covenant Publications, 2014

there, maybe He's unknowable, or maybe He doesn't care about me." This type of thinking can be deadly and can stop us in our tracks.

A story that has inspired me to keep seeking no matter how I feel at the moment is the story of the great treasure hunter Mel Fisher. He spent sixteen years of his life searching for two Spanish galleons that sank during a hurricane in 1622, near Key West, Florida. Every day, regardless of his feelings and circumstances he insisted, "Today's the day!" He was continually motivated with the expectation and hope of discovery. Mel Fisher could have easily given up. He suffered many personal losses, including an accident at sea that cost the life of his son. During the search, he also endured more than 100 court battles which ultimately ended in victory in the US Supreme Court. But finally, after sixteen years of searching, Mel found what he was seeking. He discovered the ship. The *"Mother Lode"* contained more than forty tons of silver and gold, including more than 100,000 Spanish silver coins known as "Pieces of Eight." The coins, gold and silver bars, Columbian emeralds, and artifacts recovered are worth billions of dollars in today's markets.[4]

What if, however, he had given up after the first year or the fifteenth year?

In the same way, we must not give up too soon in our quest to know God. We can't throw in the towel when we don't "feel" like we're getting anywhere. This is a real challenge in our fast-paced, "instant download" culture where we feel that things are just not moving fast enough for us. Many people do not want to take the time if there is no immediate reward. The Bible speaks to this type of

---

[4] Weller, Robert, and Ernie Richards. *The Dreamweaver: The Story of Mel Fisher and His Quest for the Treasure of the Spanish Galleon Atocha.* Charleston, SC: Fletcher and Fletcher Pub., 1996.

thinking when it says, "And without faith it is impossible to please God, because anyone who comes to Him must believe that He exists and that He is a rewarder of those who earnestly seek Him" (Heb. 11:6). In our pursuit of God, we must believe that our effort will eventually be rewarded. At first, our seeking might feel like duty or a discipline, but eventually we will come to experience the joy described in Jesus' parable of the man who found the treasure in the field.

So, I encourage you to pick up the shovel and start digging; start reading the Bible slowly and contemplatively. Read the works of great Christian authors; entering into dialogue with other believers. At first, it might seem like work. You might be tempted to give up, but God is worth it. He is the most wonderful, exciting personality in the universe. As you start to get to know His heart and His faithfulness, you will begin to love Him. As you love Him, you will learn to trust Him more. As you trust Him more, you will follow Him wherever He leads. As you follow Him, you will get to know Him better … and it's an upward spiral from there.

He is the greatest treasure and well worth the search. Happy hunting!

Paying Attention to God's Voice
– Rod Reed

Hearing Voices

Have you ever been at a party and heard a familiar voice call your name? The voice isn't necessarily louder than others, but it's so familiar that it immediately brings back memories and lots of emotions. You turn around and see one of your best friends that you haven't seen in a long time. You both scream and run and hug each other.

A few years ago, I was at a conference, and in between sessions I was sitting on the floor in the lobby checking Facebook when I saw something that made me laugh out loud. As I laughed, a couple turned around and said, "Rod Reed?" I looked up to see two of my good friends from college whom I hadn't seen in more than twenty years. They knew it was me, just by the sound of my laugh! My laugh brought back memories for them, and the sound of their voices brought back memories for me. When someone important to you calls your name, you hear it differently. In their voice, your name is more than just a name. Your name carries with it a whole history of friendship and memories.

I am convinced that the God who knows us and loves us is regularly calling our names in various ways each day, trying to get our attention. He loves us so much and has so many good things that He wants to give us and talk to us about. However, we often miss out on His voice. It's not because we don't want to listen to Him, but because we haven't spent enough time with Him to recognize His voice like we remember our friend's voice or our mom's voice. My hope in this chapter is to give you some examples of how God tries to speak to us through the normal activities of everyday life, and some practical tools that you can use to learn to recognize His voice.

Waterfalls of Words

As we think about learning to recognize God's voice, two questions come to my mind. First, how much talking is God actually doing? Second, how do we learn to listen? I think the Bible addresses both questions.

With regard to the first question, we can look to Psalm 19:1-4, where the author says this:

> The heavens declare the glory of God;
> the skies proclaim the work of his hands.
> Day after day they pour forth speech;
> night after night they reveal knowledge.
> They have no speech, they use no words;
> no sound is heard from them.
> Yet their voice goes out into all the earth,
> their words to the ends of the world.

As I read these words, I'm struck by two things. The first is that God is not stingy with His words. It is not as if He is trying to hide himself from us and make us search for His words through a maze or a scavenger hunt. The psalmist says that His creation "pours forth speech" every day, and every night it "reveals knowledge." "Their voice goes out into all the earth." This seems almost excessive; waterfalls of words are flowing all around us. God wants so much for us to know Him that He designed the natural world so that it continually communicates His love and truth to us. His voice surrounds us wherever we are.

However, the other part of this passage that stuck out to me comes in verse three, where it says that the heavens "have no speech, they use no words; no sound is heard from them." That is the part that makes more sense to me. I typically don't hear voices from heaven or get lots of clear messages about God from the natural world. The world seems to contain more silence about God than word waterfalls. How do we put these things together? Is God pouring forth speech, or is He silent?

The Apostle Paul also addresses this topic in Rom. 1:20. He says, "For since the creation of the world, God's invisible qualities—His eternal power and divine nature—have been clearly seen, being understood from what has been made, so that people are without excuse."

Again, we see an example of communication through mixed methods. God's qualities are "clearly seen," yet they are invisible. From the beginning of time, He has infused the natural world with the message of His character and ability. The message is clearly seen, but many don't notice it. What is more troublesome about this passage is that in verses 18-19, Paul tells us that we are accountable for what God is saying to us:

"The wrath of God is being revealed from heaven against all the godlessness and wickedness of men who suppress the truth by their wickedness, since what may be known about God is plain to them, because God has made it plain to them."

If we don't listen to God's message, we risk His wrath. So, are there ways that we can learn to pay attention to what God is saying?

The Bible speaks to this issue, too. In three different places in the Gospels, Jesus uses a curious phrase to talk about learning to listen to his voice. In each place, he tells a version of the story that many people call the Parable of the Sower. In this story, Jesus describes how different people receive his teaching, and what they do with it. Some ignore him, while others receive his message. Of those who receive his message, some keep listening and obeying, while others stop. At the end of the story, he says, "*He who has ears to hear, let him hear.*" (Matt. 13:9, Mark 4:9, Luke 8:8) This is a strange saying. Why would Jesus put into question whether people have ears, and if they do, that they should hear? Unless we have hearing loss, don't we automatically hear, if we have ears? Actually, we don't. Probably all of us have had the experience of one of our parents asking us, "Are you listening to me?" That's because it's pretty easy not to listen, even when sound surrounds us. Jesus understands this and calls us to really hear him. In fact, Jesus follows up this story in the Luke passage by saying, "Therefore, consider carefully how you listen." This issue of listening is important. It doesn't happen automatically, so Jesus calls us to develop both the skill and the orientation to really listen to God's voice. What would that look like in normal life?

Words in the Wind

The first answer to this question is the most obvious. In this case, the Sunday School answer is a good one. We first learn to listen to God through regular reading of the Bible. Through the stories and teachings of Scripture, we learn to recognize what God's voice sounds like, just as we learned to recognize our parents' voices when they talked to us as children. As we got older, we not only recognized their voices, but we also recognized what types of things they were likely to say. We learned that our mom was not likely to tell us we could eat ice cream for breakfast and all the candy we wanted during the day. And when our older brother told us, "Mom said we could have ice cream for breakfast," we knew that he was trying to get us into trouble! Similarly, the more time we spend listening to God's voice in Scripture, the more likely we are to recognize when He is speaking to us and to determine what messages are really from Him. We start recognizing the types of things He is likely to say, as well as when people are distorting His messages.

If reading the Bible is the most obvious way to hear God's voice, learning to hear His voice through the world around us seems to take more practice. However, as we've seen through Scripture, this is one of the key ways that God tries to show us who He is. What would it look like to start paying attention to Him more in this way?

The verses from Psalm 19 tell us that the natural world is speaking all the time. What is it saying? To figure this out, we probably need to spend more time examining God's world. When we get out of our cities and neighborhoods, and turn off our phones for a while, we see the beauty of God's world. Whether you're a beach person or a mountain person, seeing the beauty of nature often brings to mind awe, gratitude, perspective, and even worship. We wonder about who could have made all of this. We consider what it says about God that nature is so diverse and extravagant in color and texture and sound. God could have just created only three or seven or twelve colors, but instead He lavished an infinite color palette upon us. He could have made a world that is flat and uniform, but instead we see hills and valleys, and different types of rocks, and trees with different styles of bark. Why was God so extravagant in his creation? When we see these things, and ask these questions, and we recognize that God is behind all of this, it should cause us to worship. We should praise God for His creativity and His extravagance and His generosity in giving us such a beautiful world.

However, when we really look and listen to nature, we also recognize more than just beauty. In the natural world, we also observe elements of God's terrible power in the winds of a tornado and the pull of a riptide. We grasp that there are consequences to foolish decisions when we sprain our ankle on unseen rocks in the rapids of a mountain creek. We see the lack of predictability in the summer thunderstorm and winter blizzard. We recognize our own smallness as we stare over the edge into a deep canyon or look up into the expanse of a clear, starry sky.

Each of these experiences can be just nature experiences, or if we learn to listen, we begin to recognize God's voice. We start to see the heavens pouring forth speech, and the creation speaking plainly about God's character and power. Our ears get tuned to God's frequency, and His voice gets clearer to us. It's not that He is speaking more, or speaking louder, or even speaking more clearly. We are just learning to listen more carefully.

Messages in the Mirror

As we learn to listen, we recognize that God isn't just speaking through the skies and the waves and the storms, and not even just through the Bible. God also speaks in the middle of life in the city, at our jobs, in the classroom, or even while we're getting ready in the morning. Two stories from students I know illustrate this point.

A few years ago, Mario (not his real name) walked into my office and I noticed something different about him. Usually, Mario had a goatee, but on that day, he was clean-shaven. I asked him what happened to the goatee, and he told me a story about listening to God. He had been reflecting a lot about his life, and had begun to realize that he had some significant areas of immaturity in his life. He said, "I realized that facial hair is a sign of manhood, and I don't think I'm acting like a man these days, so I shaved off my goatee." He went on to say that until he had resolved some of his immaturity issues, the daily act of shaving was going to be a reminder of who God wanted him to be, and the work that needed to happen to pursue that picture of manhood. Each morning while he shaved, he focused on listening to the Holy Spirit speak to him about changing core aspects of his life.

It's interesting to me that Mario learned to listen to God while he was looking in the mirror. In many ways, the mirror was "pouring forth speech day after day" in the same way that the heavens pour forth speech. God wanted to get Mario's attention about his life, and the main tool was not the Bible, or a pastor's sermon in church, or some worship music. God used the mirror, and then the act of shaving to speak to Mario. And Mario, because he had learned to recognize God's voice, was able to hear what God was trying to say to him. Mario is married now and is a father … and has a beard again.

A few months after Mario came to my office, I talked with another student who had a similar story. One Tuesday, I walked into chapel and noticed that Sarah had dyed her hair, changing it from black to almost white. When I asked her about it, she told me about recognizing God's voice of conviction. She said, "I have realized that I am very judgmental, particularly of people who dye their hair." She then proceeded to describe how she felt God wanted her to deal with her judgmental attitude was to dye her hair and experience what it's like to be judged by her appearance. When I asked her how it was going, she responded, "I hate it. I hate having to answer questions all the time, and have people look at me weird." Just like Mario, she told me how the daily routine of doing her hair, and of responding to questions about her appearance had become tools of the Holy Spirit to help her listen to God's voice. The daily looks in the mirror were helping her learn to pay attention to the Holy Spirit's voice in her life.

What interests me about both stories is that shaving and doing your hair are not inherently spiritual activities. They are routines that millions of men and women do every day around the world. But for Mario and Sarah, these daily routines became opportunities to listen to God's voice. They recognized that God was trying to speak to them, and they had learned to recognize His voice just enough to be able to hear what He was saying to them.

Sometimes we think that only "spiritual" activities can change us, and these activities usually only happen in "spiritual places." But Mario and Sarah experienced the reality of God pouring forth speech in the most normal activities of their lives. If God is constantly at work around us, trying to get our attention—and it seems He is—one of the most faithful things we can do is to learn how to pay attention and respond in practical ways.

Listening to What You Love

So, one of the questions that you might be asking is, "Where is God speaking in my life, and how do I learn to listen to him?" If you're not asking this question, I'd encourage you to start.

I've found that God tends to speak to us through the activities that are most important and common to us. In Scripture, God spoke to fishermen while they were fishing and farmers while they were farming and parents while they were caring for their children. Similarly, God will often speak to you through the things that are most important and common to you, if you learn to tune your ears to His voice. Here's an example.

I love sports. Specifically, I love the Dallas Cowboys. Being a Dallas Cowboys fan has not been easy for most of the last 20 years, and so Sunday afternoons have often been painful for me. In 2014, I found myself getting so angry about these football games that I became very grouchy with my wife and kids. As I was watching a game one night by myself (because no one wanted to watch with me), I had a very clear sense that God wanted to talk to me about my priorities and my attitudes. I realized that my love for football had gotten out of control, and it was affecting my relationships with my family, whom I love a lot more than the Dallas Cowboys. The next step was figuring out what to do about it. Again, I tried to listen to what God was saying. What happened next was unexpected. For something to change, I needed to do something that demonstrated that my family was more important than football. And so, the next week, for the first time in almost 40 years, I intentionally chose not to watch the Cowboys on TV. Missing the game was like hitting the reset button on my emotions and attitudes. I believe that God was pouring forth speech—through the Cowboys game one week, and through the blank TV screen the next week—to help me see a picture of something better that he wanted for my life and my family. And His message landed on me in ways that helped me change. I haven't given up the Cowboys forever; I've watched them almost every weekend during football season since that time. But God has reshaped the way I watch football. And He still sometimes speaks to me during games.

What are the things that you love to do? Can you start expecting that God will speak to you during those activities? One student I know loves to run, and he has learned to listen to God while he runs. It has meant that he often chooses not to listen to music as the miles go by, so that he can use that time to listen to God. A friend of mine loves movies, and finds that God speaks to her about life through Hollywood blockbusters, independent films and Oscar winners. She hears His voice because she expects that He is speaking, and is learning to pay attention. Artist friends discover that painting, photography, calligraphy, or the pottery wheel can be places where God pours forth speech. As their creativity imitates God's creativity, they find that He speaks to them through the artistic processes. There are so many ways that God speaks to us. There are so many places where He pours forth speech day and night. The places and the activities are not the important thing. The important thing is having the expectation that God is speaking, and that He wants to speak to you. When we realize that, we start to listen for what He might want to say. We realize that we have ears, and we can really listen.

My Unchanging Identity in Christ
– Lou Y. Cha

"Who am I?" As a teenager, I asked myself this question many times. When I looked in the mirror, there were things that I really liked about myself and then there were also things that I wished I could change. I struggled with my identity, especially those aspects of myself that were different from others or seemed inferior compared to others. Perhaps right now, you might be experiencing some of these very same struggles or asking this very same question.

I thought that once I grew older and became an adult, I would stop struggling with my identity. However, I have come to realize that identity is an aspect of ourselves that we will continue to search, discover, define, and refine in every stage of life. Often, we will search for identity, significance, and worth in the temporary things of this world and try to conform ourselves to the external voices of our family, our friends, the media, and society. Yet these temporal things have the power to disappoint, distort, and hinder us from discovering our true identity in Christ Jesus, which God, our Creator, has bestowed upon us.

As you read this chapter on your unchanging identity in Christ, I pray that the truths of God's Word may speak, penetrate, and take root in your heart, soul, and mind. Let these unchanging truths become the secure foundation upon which you form and shape your identity throughout the years of your life. And let God's voice be the primary voice that defines who you are.

Changing Human Identity

Before we move into the topic of our unchanging identity in Christ, let us explore some general observations about identity and identity formation. What is identity? Simply defined, identity is an accumulated perception of one's self as a human person. Identity is formed internally through progressive self-awareness, self-discovery, and self-definition, as well as externally through socialization and engagement in significant relationships and roles.

The formation of our personal identity begins early in life and evolves through all the stages of growth and development. Our identity is both predetermined and determined. It is continually being defined and refined, formed and transformed. As we interact with our environment and the significant people in our lives, we discover who we are, who we are not, and who we desire to be. Our identity is not a static component of our being but an ever-changing one.

From our earliest days as a child, we begin to identify and define ourselves by the personal name that our parents have chosen and passed down to us. Our first name becomes a symbolic representation of the self that differentiates us from others, while our last name passes on the ancestral lineage of our respective families. One of the first words that we learn to write and spell is our name. We listen attentively and respond to others when our name is called. We also introduce ourselves and are known by others through this name.

Through experiential encounters with others during the preschool and elementary years, our identity begins to expand as we consciously recognize the ways in which we are similar and dissimilar to others in our gender, natural talents, and ethnicity. Gender-wise, we begin to recognize that boys and girls are different physically, emotionally, and relationally. We may be socially taught that boys and girls should like certain things and perform certain tasks or roles. Talent-wise, we discover that each person is inherently endowed with natural talents and abilities. Each person is special in some way. Thus, we may base our elementary identity upon those talents that we possess in greater measure to or in lesser measure than others. Ethnicity-wise, we also recognize that many of our physical features (e.g., hair color, eye color, skin color) are predetermined by our ethnic ancestry and genetic DNA. We begin to realize that how we live is not the same as how others live. So, we develop an increasing cultural awareness that our country of origin and ethnic culture influence the language that we speak, the clothes that we wear, the food that we eat, the holidays that we celebrate, and the way that we look at the world and approach life.

With the onset of puberty in the teen years, our physical appearance, body image, sexuality, and social affiliations make a significant impact upon our identity. During this period of life, we will often experiment with our physical appearance (e.g., hair, make-up, clothes, piercing, tattoos) to differentiate ourselves from others and to externally express our inward self. Some of us might struggle and experiment with our sexual orientation and sexual identity. And most of us will naturally define ourselves through the social groups that we are affiliated with (e.g., school, sports, church, club, or peer group). In order to be accepted and belong, we may conform to the attitudes, behaviors, and actions of our social group. We will often allow what our peers think about us to influence who we are both positively and negatively.

As we become adults, marriage, parenting, work, personal achievements, social group affiliations, and social status can become integral parts of our identity. In marriage, we commit to take on a new role as a husband or wife, and our identity becomes intertwined with that of our spouse. In parenting, we take on the additional roles of mother or father, and or grandmother or grandfather, and our identity may become enmeshed with that of our children and grandchildren. In addition, we establish ourselves in our vocation and work and will identify ourselves by our profession. The success, wealth, position, authority, or social status and prestige that we achieve can positively influence our self-perception. Personal failures, disappointments, broken relationships, and broken dreams can negatively impact our identity.

Our human tendency is to form, shape, and define our core identity by all of these temporal aspects (e.g., name, gender, talents, ethnicity, culture, physical appearance, human relationships, roles, work, achievements, social status). When these aspects of our life disappoint, deteriorate, decline, or fail us, this can lead to fear, anxiety, frustration, anger, disappointment, and hopelessness. We can feel lost and sink into a pit of anguish and despair. To save us from such anguish, God desires for us to firmly establish our core identity upon our inherent worth and value in Christ. As Ephesians 1: 11-12, Message translation, tells us, "It's in Christ that we find out who we are and what we are living for. Long before we first heard of Christ and got our hopes up, He had His eye on us, had designs on us for glorious living, part of the overall purpose He is working out in everything and everyone." This is an eternal identity that will never change, weaken, fluctuate, nor fail us.

Unchanging Identity in Christ

Our eternal identity is the gift of God's grace. It is a constant identity that has been created, formed, shaped, and defined by none other than God Himself; our Creator and heavenly Father. This eternal identity is rooted and centered around the person and completed work of Jesus Christ. Throughout the Bible (God's sacred words), God has revealed His truths to us about our true identity in Christ. The following "I am" statements reflect these truths about your intrinsic worth, value, and identity in Christ.

I am God's masterpiece. From the beginning of time, God has revealed that it is He who is the Creator of the heavens and the earth and of all living things, including human beings (Gen. 1:1). It is God who breathes the breath of life into human beings. Job 12:10 declares, "In his hand is the life of every creature and the breath of all mankind." Acts 17:25-28 affirms that "He himself gives everyone life and breath and everything else ... For in Him we live and move and have our being." The very breath you breathe and the very life you possess is a gift from God.

As the giver of life, God created you in the image of God to fill the earth with His beauty, majesty, and glory. In Genesis 1:27, God reveals that "God created man in His own image, in the image of God He created him; male and female He created them." Genesis 9:6 reiterates that, "For in the image of God He made humanity." Being made in the image of God means that God has created you with similar capacities and character like God (e.g., thinking, reasoning, moral decision-making, creating, relating to others, loving others, caring for others, governing others).

You are God's handiwork, His masterpiece. You are fearfully and wonderfully made (Ps. 139:13-14). You were carefully formed and crafted in your mother's womb by the invisible hand of God in order to accomplish good works, which God prepared in advance for you to do (Eph. 2:10). God knows the plans and purposes He has for you. Because God made you, God knows you, God loves you, and God cares for you. You have intrinsic value and worth because you are created by God in the image of God.

I am loved by God. You are loved by God. Let me repeat that again so that your heart can grasp this eternal truth. You are loved by God. God is love and perfect love is found in Him (1 John 4:16). Human love is finite and fallible, but the love of God is infinite and infallible. Human love can disappoint you, hurt you, wound you, scar you, betray you, and sometimes abandon you. But the love of God is faithful, righteous, just, kind, forgiving, compassionate, and enduring. He will never leave nor forsake those who seek Him (Ps. 9:10). He is near to you when you are brokenhearted (Ps. 34:18). As your loving Father, He teaches you, guides you, corrects you, and disciplines you when necessary (Heb. 12:6).

His love for you is relentless and unchanging. His affections for you are unwavering. Nothing, no, nothing in heaven or on earth can separate you from the love of God that is in Christ Jesus, neither trouble nor hardship, persecution nor famine, shame nor guilt, danger nor war, death nor life, angels nor demons, the present nor the future, "nor any powers, neither height nor depth, nor anything else in all creation" (Rom. 8:35, 37). Even before you were cognizant of God's existence, God loved you and demonstrated His love for you through the life, death, and resurrection of His son, Jesus Christ (John 3:16; 1 John 4:10)

I am found in Christ. Out of God's love for you, God seeks and pursues you so that you may encounter God and receive the fullness of His presence, His promises, and His blessings. The Bible reveals an undeniable truth about us: although created in the image of God, we have all rebelled against God and fallen short of God's will and intentions for us (Rom. 3:23). Instead of worshiping the true living God who created us, we have turned to idolatry; worshiping false gods, man-made idols, even worshiping ourselves (Rom. 1:23). Instead of following and obeying God, the Shepherd of our souls (1 Pet. 2:25), "we all, like sheep, have gone astray, each of us has turned to our own way" (Isa. 53:6). Instead of living in the light of God's truth, we live in the darkness of our own depraved human knowledge and the wisdom of this world. There is no human being who is completely good, moral, or just (1 John 1:8,10). Our very nature as human beings has been corrupted by wickedness, evil, greed, immorality, and all other kinds of sins (Rom. 1:29). Thus, we are slaves to sin (Rom. 6:16-17).

Because of our fallen human nature, you and I are prodigals. Like the prodigal son of Jesus' parable (Luke 15:11-32) who ran away from his father and squandered all of his inheritance, we desire to overthrow the authority, will, and control of our heavenly Father. We want to live out our lives according to our own rules instead of living under the righteous commands of our Father. We demand our rights and claim for ourselves the riches and inheritance that we perceive rightfully belongs to us. We may run away from God our loving Father in pursuit of our own selfish desires. Yet it is God who patiently waits for us to return to Him. Even when we are lost and can't find our way, God sends His Son Jesus to seek us, to find us, and to save us from our circumstances. If you are reading this, Christ has found you. Draw near to God and He will draw near to you. Open your heart to Christ and He will come and reveal Himself to you and lead you home to your heavenly Father who loves you.

I am forgiven and freed in Christ. As our heavenly Father, God is merciful and compassionate. He longs for the return of the prodigals, the sinners, and the rebels. He welcomes us with open arms ready to receive us despite our filth, nakedness, shame or guilt. He forgives us when we confess our sins before Him. And He cleanses us and purifies us of our unrighteousness and clothes us with the righteousness of Christ (1 John 1:9).

Even when you have squandered away your life, and are destitute and desperate, if you humble yourself before God and return to Him, confessing of your sins and asking for forgiveness and restoration, God will forgive you. He is your heavenly Father who loves you. Do not let your mistakes, your sin, or your shame hold you captive. Confess them to the Lord and let God's forgiveness set you free. For Christ died to set you free so that you may live the abundant life that God has planned and purposed for you.

Through your repentance and trust in Christ, Christ sets you free from slavery to sin and the sinful nature (Acts 13:39). Christ sets you free from the power of darkness and evil, free from the evil one, free from your past mistakes and failures, free from the hurts and wounds that paralyze and imprison you, and free from fear and death (Hebrews 2:15). In Christ, you are victorious.

I am redeemed in Christ. In Psalm 107, the psalmist declares that God is good and that His love endures forever. God Almighty is your great deliverer and mighty redeemer. Even when you wander aimlessly in the desert wastelands of life—hungry and thirsty, it is God who will hear your cry and come to your rescue. God will fill you and satisfy you with the riches of His love. Even when you are imprisoned in darkness due to your rebellion against God, God will save you, bring you out of the darkness, and break the chains that imprison you. Even when you suffer because of your own foolish mistakes and face despair and hopelessness, God will heal you and rescue you. Even when you are caught in a terrifying and unexpected storm, and you are at your wits end, God will calm the raging storm within, fill your heart with peace, and guide you to safety, if you cry out to Him in faith.

God has already acted mightily on your behalf to save you from death and destruction. While you and I were yet sinners, Christ died for us (Rom. 5:8). Christ willingly sacrificed his life on the cross to pay the price for our sins against God. Even though you and I deserve death for our rebellion against God, Christ has paid the penalty for us once and for all. The blood of Christ atones for your sins, reconciles you with God, and attains forgiveness for you (Hebrews 9:12-14). If you confess with your mouth that

Jesus is Lord and believe in your heart that Jesus is the risen Son of God, then you are saved (Rom. 10:9) from the righteous judgment of God against those who continue to live in wickedness and evil. With his life, Christ has purchased you from death to eternal life (1 Corinthians 6:20).

I am resurrected in Christ. Christ redeems you in order to give you a new life consecrated unto God in true righteousness and holiness (Rom. 6:22). This is your spiritual rebirth into the living hope of Christ (1 Peter 1:3). Through the indwelling of the Spirit of God, who searches and knows the deep things of God, Christ is purifying you, healing you, and transforming you into wholeness and holiness. The Spirit will convict you of areas of your life that are displeasing to God so that you may crucify and die to your old self and allow Christ to reign supreme in all aspects of your life as your sovereign King and Master.

Through your acts of surrender to Christ, Christ will create in you a new heart to desire God and the things of God. Christ will heal your brokenness. He will renew you and restore you. In John 11:25, Jesus pronounced that, "I am the resurrection and the life." Out of your darkness, brokenness, shame, guilt, and barrenness, Christ is resurrecting newness of life into your soul, your heart, your mind, your relationships, etc. Christ will transform you in increasing measure so that you become more and more like Christ. This sanctifying work of Christ through his indwelling Spirit will continue until the fullness of Christ is manifested in you so that it is no longer you who live, but Christ who lives in you and through you. For God has resurrected you to become a living sanctuary for His presence and power. You are a dwelling place for the Spirit of God (1 Corinthians 6:19), a holy temple being built up in the fullness of Christ for the glory of God (1 Peter 2:5).

I am a child of God and co-heir with Christ. To all who believe in Christ and receive the Spirit of Christ, they are adopted by God and receive a newborn identity as children of God (Galatians 3:26). In John 1:12-13, the apostle John declares that "yet to all who did receive him, to those who believed in his name, he gave the right to become children of God children born not of natural descent, nor of human decision or a husband's will, but born of God." This adoption is the lavish outpouring of the Father's love upon those who believe in Christ (1 John 3:1).

It is the fulfillment of God's covenant promise to bless all the peoples of the earth through the offspring of Abraham (Rom. 9:8), the lineage through which Jesus was born, so that people from every nation, language, and tribe may be called "children of the living God" (Rom. 9:26). Rom. 8:15 reveals that it is the indwelling Spirit of God who "testifies with our spirit that we are God's children." Because of this adoption, you can approach God as His child and call Him, "Abba, Father."

As an adopted child of God, you are co-heir to God's promises and to His eternal kingdom in Christ (Galatians 3:9). Rom. 8:17 pronounces that, "Now if we are children, then we are heirs—heirs of God and co-heirs with Christ, if indeed we share in his sufferings in order that we may also share in his glory." Through the gospel of Christ, Christians from all people groups and nations are justified by grace and become one body with God's people Israel and sharers together in the covenant promise of eternal life (Ephesians 3:6; Titus 3:7).

I am chosen and anointed by Christ. In Luke 4:18-19, Jesus announced at the beginning of his ministry that the Spirit of God had anointed him to proclaim good news, to proclaim freedom, to heal, to liberate the oppressed, and to proclaim that the time of God's kingdom and God's favor upon humanity had come. This work of Christ is also to be the work of those who follow Christ. In John 20:21, Jesus instructed his disciples that "as the Father has sent me, I am sending you."

The apostle Peter proclaims to followers of Christ that "you also, like living stones, are being built into a spiritual house to be a holy priesthood, offering spiritual sacrifices acceptable to God through Jesus Christ" (1 Peter 2:5). In 1 Peter 2:9, Peter declares that "You are a chosen people, a royal priesthood, a holy nation, God's special possession, that you may declare the praises of Him who called you out of darkness into His wonderful light."

As a follower of Christ, you have been chosen by Christ. You have been commissioned by Christ and anointed by Christ through the power of the indwelling Holy Spirit as a royal priest, a shepherd, a humble servant, and an ambassador of Christ to boldly proclaim the good news of Jesus and to embody the love of Christ for the sake of others. You are called by Christ to live a life that is consecrated and set apart for the Lord and dedicated to service to God to proclaim, lead, guide, and disciple others to spiritual maturity in Christ according to the spiritual gifts that Christ has apportioned to you (Ephesians 4:7-13).

I am a citizen of the kingdom of God. As a follower of Christ, you are called to live as a pilgrim, a traveler, an alien, and a stranger in this world. This world is not your home. This life is not your final destination. In 2 Corinthians 5:1-10, the Bible utilizes the analogy of a tent to describe our human journey through life. This human body is an earthly tent that will one day be destroyed through tragedy, illness, and death. Yet God has prepared for us an eternal home and a spiritual body that is imperishable and full of glory and power (1 Corinthians 15:39-49). The presence of God's indwelling Spirit in us is a deposit of what is to come.

Thus, as you journey through life, you are to fix your eyes, not on the things of this world, but to fix your eyes upon Jesus and His eternal kingdom (Hebrews 12:2). You are not to live like the people of this world, seeking after worldly pleasures and worldly gain. But you are to be a light to the world (Matt. 5:14). For you are a citizen of the kingdom of God (Phil. 3:20). Your destiny is to live with God and Christ eternally in His heavenly kingdom, which God has prepared for those who love Him (Revelation 22:1-5).

Claim Your Identity

This is the eternal identity which God has sovereignly bestowed upon you through faith in Jesus Christ. Receive this identity. Claim it in the name of Jesus. The evil one desires to hide and steal this eternal identity from you so that you will continue to live in the shifting identities of this temporary life. Do not look to the things of this world to define who you are. Instead, look to Christ.

For Jesus is the visible image of the invisible God (Colossians 1:15). Through the person and life of Jesus, God has revealed to us who we are to be and how we are to live in the world. To be truly human is to be like Jesus, filled with compassion, love, mercy, righteousness, holiness, justice, humility, service, loyalty, devotion, and purpose. By our own efforts, we all fall short of who God created us to be. We become imprisoned and enslaved by our own insecurities, selfishness, greed, and idolatry. Yet through faith in Christ, Christ emancipates us to a new spiritual birth, a new life, and a new eternal identity in Christ.

Saved by His Grace
– Ted Song

Are you a Christian?

Test yourselves to see if you are in the faith; examine yourselves! Or do you not recognize this about yourselves, that Jesus Christ is in you—unless indeed you fail the test? - 2 Corinthians 13:5 -

I recently finished hosting a weeklong summer engineering academy for high school students at John Brown University. While it is always fun to watch students learn more about engineering, the best part of my week was the conversations I had with students during meal times and breaks. One conversation in particular sticks in my mind. The conversation was with a young man named Justin, who attends a public high school. I asked him to estimate how many students in his school he thought were Christians. His answer made me think. Justin told me that about half the student body would claim themselves as Christians, but from his perspective, only half of those who claim to be Christian seem to genuinely follow Jesus.

What was happening with those students who claim themselves to be Christians but, from Justin's perspective, are not following Christ? Moreover, what makes a person a Christian? Or how do we define a Christian? These are some of the important questions that we could ask ourselves.

I looked up the definition of the word "claim." The dictionary I used says that to claim is to, "assert or affirm strongly," and I think it is a good description of the word. When a person claims to be a Christian, their claim may be based on different understanding of what 'Christian' means. For example, a person could claim himself or herself to be a Christian because he or she truly believes in Jesus Christ. Alternatively, a person could claim the same thing because his or her parents are Christians. And another person could claim the same thing again because he or she attends church every Sunday. While a Christian may have Christian parents or attend church regularly, we know that the claim of being a Christian cannot be based on either of those two elements. So, how do I know that I am a Christian? I know because I experienced God's redeeming love through faith in Jesus Christ.

Claiming to be a Christian

"Not everyone who says to Me, 'Lord, Lord,' will enter the kingdom of heaven, but he who does the will of My Father who is in heaven will enter." - Matt. 7:21 -

I was born in a Christian home. Since one of my church's traditions was infant baptism, I was baptized as a baby boy. I still have the picture of my senior pastor baptizing me, and when I was growing up, I was always proud of that picture because the pastor was very famous. Growing up, somehow, that picture became the centerpiece of my confidence in my faith. When someone asked me if I was a Christian, I could give a "yes" without a pause since I knew so well that I was baptized as an infant. More so, I tried not to miss worship services on Sundays as I knew I was a Christian from birth, and I wanted to do my best to become a good believer.

If you grew up in church, you know there are so many things you can participate in as a kid. That fact applied to me as well; I was in the youth choir, I volunteered to visit nursing homes, and I did lots of evangelism just to mention a few activities. While there is nothing wrong with doing so many things as a youth, as I look back, the biggest problem I have is that all these were things I felt I had to do. I thought that I had to serve in church because I needed to be a good Christian. I thought that I needed to participate in evangelism because I was a good Christian boy. I gained some satisfaction from serving in various capacities, but at the same time, these felt like homework assignments that I had to accomplish as a believer.

In high school, I would pray before my exams so that I would do well on them and go on to one of the best colleges. I thought I had a bright future, and I wanted to become an achieved, successful, and respected man in this world. This personal agenda did not change during my college years, and I was one of the highest achieving students in the college. Everything was perfect. I did not pray or read the Bible during the weekdays, but I always wanted to go to church on Sundays because I regarded myself as a Christian. If you don't go to church on Sundays, how can you call yourself a Christian? With this attitude, I attended worship services, praying and hoping that God would help me with the things that I wanted to achieve in this world.

Maybe now you see the problem I had when I grew up. My faith was rooted in my baptism and church attendance, and just having those, obviously, was not enough to provide me great joy or happiness. I strove hard to conform to 'Christian' rules and regulations, but the path of performance proved too burdensome for my journey. As you may have guessed already, "my effort" could not carry me far. When I found greater joys in other things, such as my dream in college to become a successful businessman, I was quick to walk away from the burden that I carried of striving to be a Christian.

Lost in Church?

Jesus answered and said to him, "Truly, truly, I say to you, unless one is born again he cannot see the kingdom of God." - John 3:3 -

To pursue a graduate degree, I moved to a new place—Austin, Texas. The motivation was to keep doing well in school so I could keep working on my agenda, but God had a different plan. The church I began attending was much smaller than the one I attended previously. Everyone could see how others lived or followed Christ. Before long, my fellow church members could see how I had my own dreams for myself and was disconnected from God.

I still remember the question that one of the church leaders asked me: "Would you like to hear the gospel?" When I heard this question, I was angry as I thought that the gospel is only for non-believers. I kept thinking, and I could not understand why this leader asked me that question. In my heart, I was saying, "Do you not know who I am? I was baptized when I was born, and I have always attended worship services my whole life. Who do you think that I am?" I had my arguments that made me a believer, but my lifestyle and the decisions that I made every day could not lie. Unfortunately, at that moment, I ignored a chance to evaluate my faith and come back to Christ.

About two years later, I had an opportunity to work for a company in Korea during the summer. Near the end of that summer, I visited a church where one of my friends was a leader in the young adults' ministry. Interestingly, this church started each worship service with new believers' testimonies. I paid attention, and one of the testimonies was an eye-opening spiritual moment. A young man who gave his testimony talked about how he was lost in church! He talked about the new relationship that he now had with Jesus, and how he turned away from his sinful life to his Jesus-following life. He was weeping because of the grace he received and rejoicing for being saved by the blood of Jesus Christ. I do not remember all the details of his testimony, but one thing stuck in my head, "You can be lost in church?"

Sin Revealed

For the wrath of God is revealed from heaven against all ungodliness and unrighteousness of men who suppress the truth in unrighteousness. - Rom. 1:18 -

I came back to Austin after my internship in Korea, and I could not walk away from these questions rolling in my head. "Do I have that relationship with Jesus? Do I rejoice in Jesus for His grace? Do I know Jesus? Was I ever born again? Am I forgiven? Am I saved?" After all these years in the church, I started asking myself these really important questions, and I became desperate for the truth.

I was also being convicted as I took a look at scripture more deeply. Through God's words, I found who I truly am. I was a sinner who deserves death. Not just physical death, but eternal death, deserving the wrath of God. Of course, I always knew I was one of the sinners. Since no one is perfect, I did not think that being a sinner and sinning were problems at all. I thought I would always have Jesus who would save me. But God revealed my blindness using the light that comes through the good news of Jesus Christ; He let me know that I need His forgiveness.

As King David did not recognize his sin when he had an affair with Bathsheba until God sent the prophet Nathan to him, I did not recognize how awful a sinner I was before this revelation. I may have looked okay on the outside, but on the inside I was totally in darkness; my heart was so dirty, full of envy, arrogance, hatred… These were the things that were in my heart that no one could see but me. I had been throwing my guilty conscience to the cross and not worrying about the sins, but from reading scripture, which is living and active and sharper than any sword, I could not deny that I was the worst of the worst sinners who deserved eternal death.

Finally, I realized the truth; I don't have the right relationship with Jesus like the one the young man shared about in his testimony. Although I had heard of Jesus so many times throughout my life, I had my own image of Jesus, not the Jesus of the Bible. As I realized more about my sins against God, sin's weight on my shoulders grew exponentially. The weight of sin was something that I could never hold by myself. I needed help, a help that could change my heart to turn away from sins and love God.

I prayed, "God, I am a sinful man. I have sinned all my life. I never lived for you but for myself. I was never interested in the salvation or the cross of Jesus Christ. Now I know that I crucified Jesus on the cross. It was my sin that crucified Him on the cross. I am the worst, the worst, the worst sinner that does not deserve your grace. Can I still be saved? I'm hopeless without You. God, please save me … Save me … Please save me … I'm yours."

The Gospel

"Therefore, let all the house of Israel know for certain that God has made Him both Lord and Christ—this Jesus whom you crucified." Now when they heard this, they were pierced to the heart, and said to Peter and the rest of the apostles, "Brethren, what shall we do?" Peter said to them, "Repent, and each of you be baptized in the name of Jesus Christ for the forgiveness of your sins; and you will receive the gift of the Holy Spirit." - Acts 2:36-38 -

In Acts 2:36, Peter declares that Jesus was crucified by

the Jews. It's not that the Jews physically crucified Jesus, but it was their sin that crucified Jesus Christ. The Jews knew the story of Jesus physically being crucified by the Roman soldiers, but before hearing Peter's words, they did not understand it was their sin that crucified Christ. They were stunned and asked this question: "Brethren, what shall we do?" They were convicted and had brokenness in their heart for their sins, and they were asking for help with fear and trembling. Then, Peter answers their question in verse 38, "Repent, and each of you be baptized in the name of Jesus Christ for the forgiveness of your sins; and you will receive the gift of the Holy Spirit." Peter knew that just knowing the story of Jesus, does not forgive any sin. God used Peter to let the Jews know how they could be saved; they needed to know that they crucified Jesus on the cross, and to be forgiven, they needed to repent and be baptized in the name of Jesus Christ.

Similarly, I knew the story of Jesus but was not able to see how my sins crucified Jesus. God wanted me to see my sins and be broken for them so that I would seek the cure. Before I knew it, I was desperately seeking God's forgiveness. Once I was aware of my sin against the holy God, there was nothing left to do but to ask for His forgiveness. For my whole life, I was in the darkness, and for the first time in my life, I was looking for the light, Jesus Christ who died for sinners on the cross.

"Father God, can this be true? I am this awful sinner, but I can still be forgiven and have eternal life? Oh, my goodness, Jesus took my sin on the cross. I crucified Him, and He died for me, and He has risen from the dead! I'm forgiven because of His blood on the cross. He is my Savior! He is my Lord! He is Christ! I am saved! I am saved! I am saved!"

Through the scripture, I could hear the good news. I do not deserve salvation, and I am saved not because of my righteous works or efforts, but because of Jesus Christ who took my sins and died on the cross. Before knowing Jesus Christ, to me grace was something obvious and deserved, which makes the grace cheap. My understanding of grace contradicted the definition of grace because if I deserve grace from God, it's not grace anymore.

The New Creature Life

Therefore if anyone is in Christ, he is a new creature; the old things passes away; behold, new things have come. - 2 Corinthians 5:17 -

Since understanding that I crucified Jesus on the cross, I know God's grace is invaluable, not cheap. Before knowing Jesus, I regarded God as a loving God, but I never realized that God is also the God of righteousness. The wrath of God is revealed against sin, and I deserve that wrath, but His wrath was satisfied on the cross of Jesus Christ because He loves me. The cross of Jesus Christ was where God's love and righteousness met. I received the love of God, and, though undeserving, I am forgiven through the death and resurrection of Jesus Christ.

Now that I know Christ, my life has totally changed. I still am not perfect and I still sin, but I do not have to attend worship services or pray before meals to prove myself as a Christian. I now have a place to go and kneel down and repent for my sins. Jesus, who is faithful and righteous, is there for me when I struggle with my sins in this world. My Christian life based on my works and effort was finished when God let me know that it was my sin that crucified Jesus on the cross.

No longer do I have to attend worship services, to volunteer, to love the others, forcing myself with my own efforts to try to meet the standards that I'll never meet. Rather, now I want to live for Jesus according to His grace. I want to go to worship services and praise Him. I want to share the love of Jesus Christ with others. As long as I live here on earth, before going to heaven, I want to be His witness. I want to share the good news with my family members, my friends, and my students who may know the story of Jesus, but do not know Jesus yet. Although I crucified Jesus on the cross with my sins, God forgave me through the blood of Jesus Christ, and now I have only one reason to live: Jesus Christ who is my Savior and my Lord!

Prayer

This is the confidence which we have before Him, that, if we ask anything according to His will, He hears us. - 1 John 5:14 –

Dear Heavenly Father, thank you so much for giving us an opportunity to hear Your words. Do we know You? Do we know the cross of Jesus Christ? If there are readers who know the story of Jesus but do not know Jesus, please help them so that they would see the cross in their lives and receive forgiveness of their sins. For those who do know Jesus, please help them to remember it was Your invaluable grace that saved them from their sins. Father, through the cross of Jesus Christ, please help us so that we no longer live for ourselves, but just live for You for the rest of our lives. In Jesus' name we pray, Amen.

ABOUT KHARIS PUBLISHING

Kharis Publishing is an independent publishing house with a core mission to publish impactful books, and channel proceeds into establishing mini-libraries or resource centers for orphanages in developing countries, so these kids will learn to read, dream, and grow. Every time you purchase a book from Kharis Publishing or partner as an author, you are helping give these kids an amazing opportunity to read, dream, and grow. Kharis Publishing is an imprint of Kharis Media LLC. Learn more at: **https://kharispublishing.com**.